the essential barbecue

Fire & Smoke

whitecap

Contents

Introduction

What was once a crude way of cooking freshly killed game over a fire has evolved into a fabulous art form in its own right. Innovations in barbecuing have created nuances in the taste of meat, fish, seafood and even fruit and vegetables that have found their home in even the finest eateries in Europe.

History

Delving into the history books will reveal that early explorers noted the way in which Native North Americans would dry meat and fish on a frame fashioned from green saplings and placed over a smouldering fire. Spaniards dubbed this makeshift grill *barbacoa*, while French settlers who slowly roasted whole animals top to tail, coined the term, *barbe-a-queue*. No matter the origin of the barbecue, the sophisticated variations that have resulted from this simple, but brilliant, technique have delighted generations. Fire, often a destructive force, has a creative power in cooking; its wispy by-product, smoke, adds a whole new dimension to the pleasures of the palate.

For the sake of precision, barbecuing is distinguished from grilling and smoking in that it imparts a distinct smoky flavor to food. Experimenting with wonderful variations to all three methods of cooking, or even applying a novel seasoning to spice it up, has produced proud cooks throughout the world who boast that they have the finest fare. Debate over what constitutes authentic barbecue flavor still rages today. However, the casting vote lies with the diner who feasts on a glorious spread with all five senses reeling.

Getting started

This book has been designed to provide you with an overview of cooking with fire and smoke and, where necessary, in-depth descriptions of methods for exact results. We have scattered tips throughout these pages that will mean the difference between producing that which is simply good and delivering that which is nothing less than sensational. There is no guesswork here, but plenty of scope for imagination.

Our first section deals with choosing the right tools of the trade to give you the reward for effort that you deserve. Whether straightforward recipes or lavish affairs, selecting the right equipment is essential and knowing how to use it to its maximum effectiveness is even more so. The choice of equipment can significantly alter cooking times, hands-on labor and, most importantly, the outcome of your food. For example, did you know that lava rock in gas grills is almost impossible to clean effectively and if it has a coating of burned-on grease it can give food an unpleasant flavor? This sort of "know-how" can only come from experts in the field, and we are committed to passing it onto you.

Our second section is concerned with the fuels that power your barbecue, grill or smoker. From hardwoods to self-lighting briquettes, your choice of fuel will be influenced by the equipment you use and the taste you are trying to achieve with your chosen method.

To give you an idea of what is at stake, you will inevitably develop a bias towards hardwood chunks of hickory, alder, mesquite or applewood if you want to achieve an unmistakable smoky flavor in your cuisine. We take old- fashioned techniques and apply them to a contemporary setting to get the best of both worlds – century-tested traditions coupled with modern conveniences.

Our third section brings together your newly-acquired knowledge of tools, equipment and fuel to guide you in preparing the barbecue or grill for optimum performance. Using the direct-heat or indirect-heat method can depend on the type of food you are cooking and the "look" you want to create. For example, to seal in natural juices, opt for the direct-heat method which sears your meat with a characteristic grilled appearance. Combine your choice of cooking technique with dry spice rubs, sauces or marinades and the taste combinations are endless.

You will be thrilled by what a marinade can do to your meat to tenderize its flesh and to charge it with extravagant flavors. Whether a tangy lime-garlic combination or a smooth herbed wine marinade, our expert tips will advise you on how to handle tougher cuts and how to prevent your marinated meats from being charred on the barbecue. Knowledge is power, and we give you the power to create a meal that will have even the most jaded diner at your table engrossed in your offering.

Whether using commercial preparations or home-made concoctions, there is enough variety in *Fire and Smoke* to adapt to family meals or special occasions. We have assigned chapters to beef, lamb, pork, chicken, seafood, fruit and vegetables for quick reference.

From the not-so-humble hamburger to a gourmet salad bursting with color, we guide you each step of the way for a perfect presentation. Pork ribs never looked so irresistible and chicken fillets never tasted so fantastic when you don the chef's hat with our book in hand.

Have you ever tasted a meat. fish or seafood that was of a higher caliber than anything else that has ever passed your lips? It was more succulent than any dish you have sampled and it played sweet music to your tastebuds throughout every mouthful. Chances are, the secret to its success lied in its preparation. If some other cook can break free from the mundane, why not you? With this book, you can launch your cooking skills to exciting new heights. Follow our guidelines on smoking, including cold smoking and smoke cooking, or our instructions on curing or cooking with brines and you will be hooked. You will discover new twists to the flavors and aromas of many foods, including venison, shellfish, turkey, duck and ham, that you could have never dreamed possible. You will "go gourmet" in no time and you may never have to visit the meat section of a delicatessen ever again.

The beauty of developing a working knowledge of cooking is that it provides enough room for experimentation that may even lead you to unearthing the next family favorite. It is this trial by fire and smoke that has created regional flavors made famous by the proverbial grapevine. Your search for a wonderful new experience has lead you here, so may your curiosity turn to elation, and with our help, may your cooking be the talk of the town!

Basting Brush

There is no need to splurge on fancy wood-handled brushes. The cheaper version works just fine for outdoor use. Basting brushes should have long handles so that you don't burn yourself while basting.

Charcoal Rails

Designed to hold charcoal in even piles on each side of the drip pan, charcoal rails are really a bit of an extravagance. The sides of the drip pan can do just as good a job holding the charcoal in place.

Drip Pan

A drip pan is essential for the indirect-heat method of cooking (see page 14). Your best bet is to purchase a disposable aluminium pan — a 2-3in (5-7.5cm) deep rectangle — and throw it out after each use.

Grill Brush

This inexpensive tool is a must for proper grill care. Brush grill before oiling, and after cooking, while the grill is still hot, to remove any food particles or burned-on grease. If you follow this procedure consistently, you won't have to wash the grill with cleanser, which ruins the seasoning.

Hinged Wire Basket

These baskets hold fish fillets, hamburger patties, or bread between two grills secured by a latch. Simply place the food inside the basket and place the basket over the heat. When one side is done, flip it over. It is a good idea to lightly oil the basket before placing food inside.

Instant-Read Thermometer

Old style thermometers take too long to work to provide accurate cooking temperatures for grilled foods. The instant-read versions provide an accurate picture of the progress within five seconds of insertion.

Roast Racks

Made of aluminium or stainless steel, V-shaped roast racks do an excellent job holding large pieces of meat or poultry together as they cook. If you use one while cooking with indirect heat, you don't need to turn the meat at all; it cooks evenly on all sides.

Skewers

Metal and bamboo are common skewer materials. Metal skewers, of course, never burn up, but you do have to wash them. You need to soak bamboo skewers in water for 15 to 30 minutes before use to prevent their burning. If you are fortunate enough to have rosemary growing nearby, try using these branches for skewers. Remove the needles and soak the branches in water for 30 minutes. They imbue the skewered food with a pungent rosemary flavor.

Spatula

Take the time to find an offset stainless steel spatula with a blade 5 to 6in (12.5-15cm) long – the kind professional chefs use. The advantage of the long blade is that it will slide under most chops and fish fillets completely so that they won't tear or stick when being flipped over. Stainless steel will never rust and is easy to care for.

Spray Bottle

With the advent of kettles and gas grills, there aren't many fire flare-ups anymore. But always keep a spray bottle filled with water next to your grill, just in case of an emergency.

Tongs

Tongs are probably the most useful and versatile grill tool that you can buy. Use a pair that is at least 12 inches (30cm) long and spring loaded. It's not a bad idea to have two pairs, one to move hot charcoal around and one to use with food. (Of course, you can get by with one pair – you will just have to keep washing it off every time you use it to move charcoal.)

Fuels

Shopping for fuel in a well-stocked market can be quite a confusing experience. Traditional charcoal briquettes are now surrounded by many different competing fuels. Mesquite charcoal, hardwood charcoals, hardwood-flavored charcoals, "self-lighting" briquettes and a number of different types of smoke-creating hardwood chips, chunks, and sawdust all crowd the shelf. They all work well in the right situation. You must judge what will work best for you.

Charcoal Briquettes

Charcoal briquettes are made from wood chips smoldered into carbon, then bound together with fillers and starch and pressed into a uniform shape. Self-lighting briquettes are formed by the addition of petroleum products. Before beginning to cook over any briquettes, wait until they are completely coated with a thin layer of gray ash. This means that all the additives have burned off. Long, slow cooking requires that you replenish your fire with more briquettes, so you will be faced with the dilemma of how to add fresh briquettes without adding chemical fumes from the additives to your food. One solution is to start your second set of coals in a charcoal chimney — a large, vented metal can — and add them to your grill after they are covered with gray ash. A distinct advantage of charcoal briquettes is that they burn evenly and consistently. For an average fire that lasts about an hour, count out 30 to 40 briquettes. Plan on adding 16 to 20 for each additional hour.

Mesquite Charcoal

Mesquite is a scrub hardwood tree that covers the arid plains of the Southwest of America and Mexico.
It has long been used in those areas as a fuel for outdoor cooking and is rapidly becoming the most popular outdoor cooking fuel source across the country. Mesquite charcoal is simply mesquite that has been carbonized by slow smoldering in controlled conditions. There are no additives or fillers of any kind. The advantage of mesquite is that it burns much hotter than charcoal briquettes and most other hardwood charcoals. As a result, you don't have to use as much, and the high cooking temperature produces a much tastier product. Mesquite also provides a subtle smoky flavor that is not nearly as pronounced as that of fruitwoods, oak, or hickory. Leftover pieces of mesquite charcoal can be reused, something that can't be said for charcoal briquettes. Light mesquite as you would any other charcoal, but be particularly careful about high winds or nearby trees. Mesquite charcoal pops and crackles a lot when first lit, and can eject burning embers into the air. Extra supervision is required.

Hardwood Charcoals

Although not nearly as prevalent as mesquite charcoal, other hardwoods are carbonized in the same manner as mesquite to form excellent fuel sources. The advantage of hardwood charcoals is that they provide a flavorful smoky complement to your food, the disadvantages are scarcity, price, and, most significantly, the inability to burn as hot as mesquite. Try using mesquite charcoal as your fuel source and presoaked hardwood chunks as your smoke source.

For the average fire, use between 3 and 4 lbs (1.5 and 2 kilos) of either hardwood charcoal in your grill. You may need more or less, depending on the size of the charcoal. (Some times during shipping the charcoal breaks up into tiny pieces, which burn quickly.) Add an additional 1 to 2 lbs (500g to 1kilo) of charcoal hourly to maintain the fire.

Woods

Use oak, hickory, cherry, apple, mesquite, or alder as a wood for outdoor cooking. Be aware, however, that although a wood-burning barbecue is romantic, it doesn't make much sense. Wood takes a considerable time to burn down to usable coals, and wood coals don't last as long as either charcoal briquettes or hardwood charcoal. With wood you end up waiting twice as long to cook, and then your fire goes out sooner. Instead of using these woods as your major fuel source, use the smaller pieces as kindling, and cut the remainder into 1in (2.5cm) chunks to add a smoky complement to your fire. Never use a softwood for either smoking or as a fuel; the thick resins produce a distinctly unpleasant aftertaste. Be careful about burning scrap wood. Pressure-treated lumber (the type of wood used in outdoor construction), for instance, contains chemicals that can be toxic.

Hardwood Chunks and Sawdust

Food cooked over hardwood has a distinctive smoky flavor. Hickory, alder, mesquite, and applewood are the most popular and available woods.

If you use a gas grill, hardwood chips work better than chunks. Select pieces $1/2$ to 1in (1 to 2.5 cm) thick and soak them in water for at least 30 minutes before you use them. Place an old aluminium pie pan over the gas heating elements toward the back corner of your grill before you turn it on, and place the water-soaked chips in the pan. As the grill heats up, the chips will begin to smolder. You may experience flare-ups from the chips if you cook with high heat, so have your spray bottle ready. The only limitation of this method is that the chips tend to burn quickly. You'll have to monitor the progress and replenish the chips as necessary, but don't put too many on at once lest you extinguish your fire.

For the gas grill, hardwood sawdust works as well or better than hardwood chips. Easy to ignite, sawdust provides a consistent, flavorful smoke. To use, place sawdust in an old pie pan and place directly on top of lava rocks or flavorizer bars. Turn gas burners to high until sawdust just blackens and begins to smolder. Immediately turn burner underneath pan off. Replenish sawdust as needed. Hardwood sawdust is available at lumber mills and specialty cookware stores.

Fresh Herbs and Citrus Rinds

Thyme, bay leaves, rosemary, oregano and marjoram are particularly well suited to flavoring your fire. Chose one type of herb and simply moisten it with water (use wine or liquor to moisten it for an added taste treat), and toss it onto the coals right before you put food on the grill. Try lemon, orange or lime rinds as well. Add them one at a time, with or without a complementary fresh herb. Be careful not to directly inhale the fumes of burning herbs or fruit rinds, however–they can be rather powerful.

Fire Starting

Whatever method you use, allow about 30 to 45 minutes for your fire to start. Be sure to follow all the Tips for Safe Grilling. The idea is to start a fire in your grill, not in your house.

Kindling

Starting a fire with kindling is probably the most individual and ritual-laden method. Although each fire starter has a unique style, the basic method is to start with a few sheets of your favorite newspaper and crumple them loosely or twist them into "logs." Place these logs in the bottom of your grill, and then place a handful of dry kindling on top. Place five or six briquettes on top of the kindling. Light the newspaper and hope for the best. If the briquettes do not light, add more newspaper and kindling until they do. Once the briquettes light, add more briquettes on top until you have a fire of the desired size. Everyone seems to have their own ratio of newspaper to kindling to briquettes. Just do what works for you.

Electric Starter

Electricity is certainly the easiest and most foolproof means of starting a fire. Check the manufacturer's recommendations for starting a fire with an electric starter in your grill. In most cases, the instructions tell you to arrange your briquettes in a pile on top of the starter, plug it in, and let it go to work. In about 10 minutes, your briquettes should be started. Don't leave your starter in any longer, or the heating element will be damaged by lengthy exposure to high heat. The only disadvantage to this fire-starting method is that you need to be near an electrical outlet.

Charcoal Chimney

The simplicity and ease of charcoal chimneys make them a wonder to watch. A charcoal chimney is nothing more than an open-ended sheet-metal cylinder vented at the lower end, with a grate about 4 inches (10cm) from the bottom to set the charcoal briquettes on. To use, simply crumple several sheets of newspaper and place them under the grate. Fill the chimney with charcoal briquettes, and place in the bottom of the grill and light the paper. In about 10 minutes the briquettes will begin to smolder. Once all the briquettes are well ignited, pour them out of the chimney into the bottom of your grill.

A charcoal chimney is also the answer when you will be using your grill for several hours and don't want to replenish your fire with "raw" charcoal briquettes because of the fumes they emit when they just start to burn. Simply set the chimney on an old pie pan on a concrete surface and light more charcoal. When the briquettes are ready, pour them onto your existing fire.

You can make your own charcoal chimney by cutting the top and bottom off a coffee can and making a vent in the bottom with a can opener. If you buy a ready-made chimney, you will find that it is inexpensive and has the added benefits of a wooden handle and a grate to set the charcoal on.

Lighter Fluid

Follow all safety procedures listed on the can when using lighter fluid. Never squirt the fluid directly onto a burning fire. The flame can easily travel back up the stream and ignite your hands and arms, not to mention the can itself! Never use gasoline, naphtha, paint thinner or kerosene – they are too flammable for this purpose. Use only a product specifically labelled as lighter fluid.

How Much Fire?

When determining the size of your fire, first imagine the cooking surface that the food requires. Spread the briquettes out on a single layer to cover an area about 1in (2.5cm) past the edges that you have imagined. Now add about half again as much charcoal, and you should have enough for an hour's worth of fire. Usually 30 to 40 briquettes are sufficient to cook food for four people. If you are making a fire for slow cooking using the indirect-heat method (see page 14), use about 25 briquettes on each side of the grill. Plan on adding 8 to 10 briquettes to each side for every hour of additional cooking time.

When is the Fire Ready?

It usually takes between 30 and 45 minutes for a fire to be ready for cooking. Never cook over a fire until the briquettes are covered with a light ash and are no longer flaming. Cooking over a direct flame only burns the outside of your food, leaving the inside raw. Your hand is probably the best judge of when a fire is ready. Hold your hand flat over the fire at grill height. You will be able to hold your hand over a very hot fire for about 2 seconds. If the fire is hot, you can hold your hand above it for 3 to 4 seconds. If you can hold it any longer than that, you have let the fire die down too much. Add more briquettes and let it build up again. A very hot fire is ideal for the direct-heat method of cooking (see page 13); a medium to hot fire is desirable for the indirect-heat method (see page 14). Once your fire is ready, carefully add hardwood chips or fresh herbs. Put the grill in place and let it heat up for 4 to 5 minutes before putting on food.

Preparing the Grill

Always arrange the fire so that there are areas of the grill with no fire under them. If some of your food is done sooner than others, move it to these cooler spots to keep finished food warm while the remainder of the meal cooks.

Brush the grill lightly with oil right after you put it in place over the fire. To do this, moisten a paper towel with oil. Using tongs held in a fireproof mitt-clad hand, rub the oil from the towel onto the grill. This will help prevent food from sticking to the grill and will also keep the grill seasoned.

Always keep the grill clean. The best method is to quickly brush the excess food off with a grill brush immediately after you remove the food. This way the remaining fire will burn off any lingering bits, and you won't have to resort to soap and water, which would ruin the seasoning of the grill surface. If you do not have a grill brush use a crumpled wad of aluminium foil held by tongs.

Have all your grill tools ready and available before you light your fire. Tongs, mitts, and spray bottle are particularly important to have at your fingertips.

Have extra charcoal available. There is nothing more frustrating than discovering that your fire is dying before dinner is ready and there is no more charcoal.

Outdoor Cooking Methods

With the advent of covered grills, a whole new world of barbecuing opened up. Foods can now be slowly roasted over indirect heat so that they become tender and stay moist during cooking. Whether to use indirect-heat cooking or traditional grilling over direct heat depends on the type of food to be cooked and the result desired.

Direct-Heat Method

Use the direct-heat cooking method to sear foods to seal in their natural juices and to give the characteristic grilled look. Foods that are low in fat, such as poultry and fish, and foods that don't take very long to cook are ideal choices for this method. Hamburgers, chops, vegetables, skewered items, and fish fillets all fall within this category.

If using charcoal, start your fire as described on page 9. After 30 to 45 minutes, when the coals have a light gray ash covering, spread them out one briquette deep so that you have an even cooking source. Place your grill over the coals and let it heat up for 4 to 5 minutes. If you are using pre-soaked hardwood chips or chunks or moistened fresh herbs, spread them out over the coals right before placing food on the grill. The wood will immediately begin to smolder. Now you are ready to cook. When using a kettle-shaped grill, keep the lid closed for the duration of cooking; regulate the heat by adjusting the upper and lower vents. The beauty of this system is the total lack of flare-ups, even though the food is cooking at a very high temperature and fat is dripping onto the coals. The fat vaporizes as it hits the coals, imparting a desirable smoky flavor to the food, but the fat doesn't have enough oxygen to ignite into an undesirable flame. Also, the heat circulation in the kettle-shaped grill is excellent, cooking the food on top as well as on bottom. You still need to flip the food over due to the short cooking time, but it does cook faster and more evenly inside a kettle. So it is very important that the lid stay closed except when you need to baste, add coals, check the food, or turn it over. Otherwise, leave the grill alone and let it cook.

If you are using a gas grill, turn all three burners to high and close the lid. Your grill should be sufficiently hot enough to cook on in about 10 minutes. Depending on the food being cooked and the desired effect, you can leave the temperature on high while cooking or turn down one or more burners. There is a nearly immediate response to the burner temperature controls, so experiment to find the exact temperature you want.

LET'S HAVE BEEF
ON THE GRILL

Beef Grill

The tenderness of a cut of beef determines the method of cooking to use. Tender cuts can be cooked directly over high heat. The internal fat marbling will keep the meat moist as the outside chars into a crisp, succulent crust. These cuts come primarily from the loin, which is divided into the tenderloin, sirloin strip, and sirloin butt.
The most common cuts from the loin include New York strip steak, T-bone steak, porterhouse steak, club steak, top-sirloin steak, filet mignon, chateaubriand, tournedos and rump steak.
All these cuts are tender enough to cook without a marinade, but you can use a marinade if you want to imbue extra flavor. Steak cuts from the prime rib can also be grilled over direct heat. These steaks are variously called rib eyes, delmonicos, and market steaks and are the identical cut of meat.

Other beef cuts need either a marinade to tenderize the cut for direct-heat cooking or they should be cooked over indirect heat. These cuts come from the chuck, rib, cross rib, shank, flank, or leg.

When Meat is Done

Experience is the greatest teacher for determining when meat is adequately cooked. You can also use the hand test as described below, as a guide to when meat is done.
If you need to verify your sensibilities with a thermometer, use the following temperatures as rough guidelines:

Rare:	115° to 129°F (46° to 54°C)
Medium rare:	130° to 135°F (54° to 57°C)
Medium:	140° to 145°F (60° to 63 °C)
Medium well:	150° to 155°F (66° to 68°C)
Well done:	160° to 170°F (71° to 77°C)

Hand Test: Let one hand dangle freely, relaxing it completely. With the forefinger of the other hand, touch the meaty area between your thumb and forefinger. This is the way a piece of meat cooked rare should feel.

Make a loose fist with your hand. Touch the same place again. This is a medium cooked feel.

Tightly clench your fist. Touch the same place again and this is the way a well-done piece should feel.

Hot herbed beef salad

Method:

1 Place the steaks in a shallow dish. Mix together the garlic, chilli, oil, salt and pepper and pour over the steaks. Cover and stand 30 minutes.

2 Heat the barbecue grill bars to high and oil the bars. Sear meat 2 minutes on each side then turn down heat a little or move steaks to cooler part of barbecue and cook for 8 minutes on each side. Brush with marinade during cooking. Rest 5 minutes before slicing.

3 Slice meat thinly and arrange on platter lined with salad greens. Mix dressing ingredients together and pour over the beef. Serve immediately with barbecue toast.

Serves 6

Photograph page 18

Ingredients:

2 boneless beef sirloins,
1in (2.5 cm) thick
$^1/_2$ tsp crushed garlic
1 tsp chopped chilli
2 tsps oil
salt, pepper
mixed salad greens for serving
Herb Dressing
2 tsps basil pesto (store bought)
1 tsp chopped chilli
1 tbsps chopped parsley
$^1/_2$ cup chopped shallots
$^1/_2$ cup olive oil
$^1/_4$ cup vinegar

Spiced beef and carrot burgers

Method:

1 Preheat the grill to medium. Place all the ingredients in a large bowl and mix together well.

2 Shape the mixture into 4 round flat burgers, using your hands. Grill for about 10-15 minutes, until the burgers are lightly browned and cooked to your liking, turning once.

Note: These healthy burgers will be popular with all the family. Try serving them in buns piled high with crisp salad leaves, slices of tomato and tangy relish.

Serves 4

Photograph page 17

Ingredients:

1 lb extra lean ground beef
2 carrots, coarsely grated
1 cup mushrooms, finely chopped
1 large onion or 3 shallots,
finely chopped
1 cup fresh whole-wheat
breadcrumbs
2 tbsps tomato paste
1 medium egg, lightly beaten
1 clove garlic, crushed
2 tsps ground cumin
2 tsps ground cilantro
1 tsp hot chilli powder
black pepper

Deluxe hamburgers

Ingredients:

Burger Patties
2¼ lbs ground beef
1 large onion, grated or processed
½ cup dried breadcrumbs
½ tsp salt
¼ tsp pepper
3 tbsps barbecue sauce
2 tbsps water
Buns and suggested fillings
14 hamburger buns
softened butter for spreading
1 lettuce, separated into leaves,
washed and drained
1 bunch arugula (rocket), washed &
drained
2 large onions, thinly sliced and
cooked on the hotplate
cheese slices
1 bottle ketchup
1 jar vegetable relish of your choice

Method:

1 Combine all the ingredients for the burger patties, knead with hands to distribute evenly and make the texture finer. Rest for 20 minutes in the refrigerator. With wet hands, shape into 14 flat patties about 3in (8cm) in diameter.

2 Heat barbecue to hot, oil the grill bars, place on the patties and cook for 5-6 minutes on each side, brush with a little oil as they cook.

3 Split the buns and lightly spread with softened butter. Place buttered side down on hotplate and toast to golden color.

To Assemble: Place a lettuce leaf on bottom half of bun, top with cooked patty, tomato sauce, onions, cheese slice, arugula leaf and your choice of pickle or relish. Top with remaining bun. Have fun around the barbecue while creating a deluxe hamburger.

Serves 14   *Photograph page 21*

Herb crusted steak

Ingredients:

4 top-sirloin steaks (10 -12 oz each)
2 to 3 tbsps olive oil
3 tbsps Spice Rub for Meat (page 15)
oil, for grill
4 tbsps unsalted butter

Method:

1 Lightly coat steaks with olive oil, then massage meat with spice rub until well coated. Cover and let rest for at least 1 hour at room temperature to allow spices to imbue meat with flavor.

2 Prepare fire for direct-heat method of cooking (see page 13). If using a gas grill, use a hardwood sawdust for a smoky flavor complement. If using charcoal, add pre-soaked hardwood chunks.

3 When fire is very hot, place steaks on oiled grill and cook for 3 to 5 minutes on each side (depending on thickness of steak and the degree of doneness desired). Keep the lid closed during cooking. Baste the steaks once on each side with butter. The spice rub will blacken during cooking, forming a delicious and pungent herb crust. Remove from fire and serve immediately.   *Serves 4*

Toasted steak sandwiches

Method:

1 Cut the steak into 4 or 5 pieces and pound with a meat mallet until thin. Place in a non-metal container. Mix the lemon juice, garlic, salt, pepper and oil together and pour over the steaks. Coat both sides and marinate for 30 minutes at room temperature.

2 Soften the butter and spread a thin coating on both sides of the bread.

3 Heat barbecue until hot and oil the grill bars and hotplate. Place onions on the hotplate. Toss and drizzle with a little oil as they cook. When beginning to soften, push to one side and turn occasionally with tongs. Place toast on hotplate and cook until golden on both sides. Place steaks on grill bars and cook 2 minutes on each side.

4 Assemble sandwiches as food cooks by placing steak and onions on one slice of toast, topping with a good squirt of steak sauce and closing with second slice of toast.

Serves 4–5

Ingredients:

1 lb boneless sirloin steak
2 tbsps lemon juice
1 tsp crushed garlic
salt and pepper
1 tbsp oil
butter for spreading
10 slices toasted bread
2 large onions, thinly sliced
1 tbsp oil
steak sauce of choice

Perfect sirloin steak

Ingredients:

4 sirloin steaks
2 tsps crushed garlic
2 tsps oil
salt and pepper
Garlic Butter
4 tbsps butter
1 tsp crushed garlic
1 tbsp parsley flakes
2 tsps lemon juice
mix all ingredients together
and serve in a pot with a spoon

Method:

1   Bring the steaks to room temperature. Mix garlic, oil and salt and pepper together. Rub onto both sides of the steak. Stand for 10-15 minutes at room temperature.

2   Heat the barbecue until hot and oil the grill bars. Arrange the steaks and sear for one minute each side. Move steaks to cooler part of the barbecue to continue cooking over moderate heat, or turn heat down. If heat cannot be reduced then elevate on a wire cake rack placed on the grill bars. Cook until desired doneness is achieved. Total time: 5-6 minutes for rare, 7-10 minutes for medium and 10-14 minutes for well done. Turn during cooking.

3   Serve on a heated steak plate and top with a dollop of garlic butter. Serve with potatoes.

Serves 4

LET'S HAVE LAMB
ON THE GRILL

Lamb Grill

Lamb is a natural for grilling because excess lamb fat, which can be quite objectionable, drips off during cooking and the remaining fat develops a wonderful charred flavor.

Rib and loin chops are the most popular cuts for grilling, and butterflied leg of lamb is the all-time classic grilled roast. The chops are tender enough as they are; the leg of lamb needs a marinade to tenderize it. If you want to buy meat for skewers, use chunks from the shoulder or leg. Be sure to marinate them for a tender and flavorful kabab.

Lamb satays

Method:

1 Cut the lamb into $^1/_5$ in (.5cm) cubes. Place into a non-metal bowl and stir in $^3/_4$ cup of marinade. Cover and marinate for half to one hour, or longer in the refrigerator.
Soak the skewers in hot water for $^1/_2$ hour

2 Thread 2 or 3 lamb strips onto each skewer, using a weaving action. Spread to cover $^2/_3$ of the skewer only.

3 Heat barbecue until hot. Place an overturned wire-cake rack over grill bars to prevent marinade charring the hot grill. Arrange the skewers in rows on the wire rack and cook for approximately 8-10 minutes, turning frequently. Brush remaining marinade from the bowl over the lamb during cooking.

4 Thin down the remaining marinade with extra coconut milk, place in a heatproof bowl and heat on the barbecue. Remove skewers to a platter and drizzle immediately with the heated marinade.

Serves 6–8   *Photograph page 25*

Ingredients:

4$^1/_2$ lbs boned shoulder of lamb
1 cup Satay Marinade
bamboo skewers, soaked in water
Dipping Sauce
$^1/_4$ cup Satay Marinade
(see page 124)

Lamb and salsa pitas

Method:

1. Cut lamb into $^1/_2$ in (1cm) cubes. Place in a bowl and add lemon juice, salt, pepper, oil and garlic. Cover and marinate at room temperature for 20 minutes. Thread onto skewers.

2. Heat the barbecue and oil the grill bars. Place the salsa into a foil or metal container and place at side of barbecue to heat a little.

3. Cook lamb skewers for 3-4 minutes each side. Halve the pita bread and cook for 2 minutes on the barbecue. Open the pita, fill with lettuce, lamb (skewer removed) and top with heated salsa.

Serve immediately.

Serves 6   *Photograph page 27*

Ingredients:

$^1/_2$ leg of lamb
1 tbsp lemon juice
salt and pepper
2 tsps oil
1 tsp crushed garlic
bamboo skewers, soaked
1$^1/_4$ cups tomato salsa
6 pack pita bread
3 cups shredded lettuce

Cajun cutlets

Method:

1 Beat the butter to soften and mix in 1½ teaspoons of the Cajun seasoning and the chopped chilli. Place butter along the center of a piece of plastic wrap or greaseproof paper to .5 in (1cm) thickness. Fold plastic wrap over the butter then roll up. Smooth into a sausage shape and twist ends. Refrigerate to firm.

2 Trim the cutlets if necessary and snip the membrane at the side to prevent curling. Flatten slightly with the side of a meat mallet. Mix together 1½ teaspoons of the Cajun seasoning and olive oil, then rub mixture well into both sides of the cutlets. Place in a single layer onto a tray, cover and stand 20 minutes at room temperature, or longer in the refrigerator.

3 Heat the barbecue or electric barbecue grill to high. Place a sheet of parchment paper on the grill bars, making a few slashes between the bars for ventilation. Place cutlets on grill and cook for 3 minutes each side for medium and 4 minutes for well-done. When cooked, transfer to a serving plate and top each cutlet with a round slice of Cajun butter. Serve immediately with vegetable accompaniments. (see vegetable section page 70)

Serves 4–6

Ingredients:

½ cup butter

3 tsps Cajun seasoning

1 small red chilli, seeded and chopped

12 lamb cutlets

1 tbsp olive oil

28

Mini lamb roast with barbecued noodles

Method:

1. Tie the roast with kitchen string to give it a higher shape. The roast has a half moon shape and the outer edges will dry if roast is not tied.

2. In a glass bowl, mix remaining ingredients together. Drop in the lamb and turn to coat on all sides. Marinate for 1 hour at room temperature, or longer in the refrigerator.

3. Cook as follows:

   Kettle or Hooded Gas Barbecue – Prepare barbecue for indirect heat. Place lamb over drip tray in center of barbecue to use indirect heat, cover with lid or hood and cook for 35-40 minutes. There is no need to turn. Or, place lamb in foil tray in same position on rack so cooking juices will be retained. Brush with marinade as it cooks and turn once or twice.

Barbecued Noodles:

1. Rinse noodles in hot water and separate. Drain very well. Mix cilantro, feta, garlic and chilli to a paste.

2. Heat the barbecue hotplate or use a tin baking dish on grill plate. Oil hot plate or dish, add the noodles and toss around while adding the cilantro paste. Mix well and heat through.

3. Place on serving plate or platter.

4. Slice lamb and arrange over noodles. Drizzle with any remaining pan juices.

Serves 4

Ingredients:

1 small lamb roast, boned
2 tbsps chopped
fresh cilantro
1 tsp crushed garlic
1 tbsp lemon juice
salt, pepper
1 tbsp oil

Barbecued Noodles
1 lb Hokkien noodles
1 tbsp chopped fresh cilantro
1/2 cup feta cheese, crumbled
1 tsp crushed garlic
1/2 tsp chopped chilli
(optional)

Barbecued leg of lamb in paper

Ingredients:

4¹/₂ lbs leg of lamb
2 tsp salt
1 tsp pepper
¹/₂ cup lemon juice
2 tbsps freshly crushed garlic
Romano or Parmesan cheese
cut into 8 x ¹/₄in (.5cm) cubes
³/₄ cup sun-dried tomato pesto
2 sheets parchment paper, oiled
1 sheet butcher's paper, oiled on both sides

Method:

1 Wash the lamb and pat dry. Make about 8 incisions on each side of the lamb with the point of a small knife. Place lamb in a suitable non-corrosive dish, rub all over with salt and pepper and pour over the lemon juice, allowing the juice to enter the incisions. Stand 30 minutes. Push a ¹/₂ teaspoon of crushed garlic into each incision, followed by a cheese cube. Rub all over with sun-dried tomato pesto. Wrap the lamb in the 2 sheets of oiled parchment paper and then wrap into a parcel with the butcher's paper. Tie with kitchen string.

2 Prepare Kettle or Gas Hooded Barbecue for indirect heat on medium-high. Place the lamb parcel onto oiled grill bars over the drip tray and cook for 2 hours. Turn lamb after 1 hour. When cooked, remove from barbecue and rest for 20 minutes before removing from paper and carving. Take care when opening parcel that any juices are collected in a bowl. Reheat juices and serve with the carved meat.

3 Serve with a mild mustard, a green salad and garlic bread.

Serves 6 to 8

Lamb fillets with salsa pilaf

Method:

1   Trim the lamb fillets, removing the fine silver membrane. Place in a dish and add garlic, lemon juice, oil, salt and pepper. Cover and stand 30 minutes. Boil salted water and cook the rice for about 15 minutes, until rice is tender. Drain well and keep hot. Heat a small saucepan, add pine nuts and shake over heat until they colour. Add the salsa and raisins and heat through.

2   Heat the barbecue grill plate and oil lightly. Set at medium-high. Place lamb on grill and cook 6-8 minutes, turning to cook on all sides. Cook longer for well done. Rest 5 minutes before slicing in $1/2$ in (1cm) slices.

3   To Serve: Using a cup or mold, form a mound of rice on the plate. Pour salsa over the rice and arrange lamb slices at base of rice mold.

Serves 4-5

Ingredients:

2 lamb fillets (about $1^1/_2$ lbs)
$^1/_2$ tsp crushed garlic
1 tbsp lemon juice
2 tsps olive oil
salt & pepper
Salsa Pilaf
1 cup uncooked rice
6 cups boiling water, mixed with 1 tbsp salt
$^1/_4$ cup pine nuts, toasted
1 $^1/_4$ cups tomato salsa
2 tbsps raisins

Glazed pork spare ribs

Ingredients:

2 lbs pork spare ribs
(American-Style)
Soy and Honey
Marinade (page 124)

Method:

1   Place spare ribs on a large sheet of heavy-duty foil and cover both sides generously with marinade. Wrap into a double-folded parcel, making sure all joins are well-sealed to prevent leakage. Stand for at least half an hour before cooking. Place in refrigerator if not to be cooked immediately.

2   Prepare the barbecue for direct-heat cooking. Place a wire cake-rack on the grill bars to stand 1in (2.5cm) above the bars. Place ribs in the foil parcel on the rack and cook for 10 minutes each side.

3   Remove to a plate, discard foil, then return ribs to rack. Continue cooking, brushing with fresh sauce or marinade and turning each minute until ribs are well browned and crisp (about 10 minutes). Total cooking time is approximately 30-35 minutes.

Note: Ribs may be cooked by indirect heat in a hooded barbecue. There is no need to wrap in foil. Place over indirect heat after marinating. Brush and turn frequently with lid down for 1 hour or more. Cooking in the foil over direct heat cuts cooking time in half.

Serves 4   *Photograph page 36*

Gorgonzola pork chops

Method:

1 If possible, have a butcher cut extra thick center-cut pork chops (about 1 inch (2.5cm) thick) and make a pocket in them for stuffing. Use a high quality Italian sausage made with fennel and garlic. If you can't find the sausages in your local market, see the Special Note on page 108.

2 In a medium skillet on the range, saute sausage over medium heat until just done (about 10 minutes). Drain and transfer to a medium bowl. Add pine nuts, tomatoes and Gorgonzola and mix well. Cover and refrigerate until cold (about 30 minutes). Place stuffing into pocket of each chop and seal pockets with toothpicks.

3 Prepare fire for direct-heat method of cooking (see page 12). Rub meat with olive oil; season with salt and pepper. When fire is ready, place chops on oiled grill. Cook over hot fire until just firm to the touch 145°F (63°C) on a meat thermometer), about 10 minutes per side.

Serves 4

Ingredients:

$^3/_4$ lb mild or hot
Italian sausage, removed
from casings
$^1/_4$ cup pine nuts, toasted
2 tbsps sun-dried tomatoes
packed in olive oil, ground
$^1/_2$ lb Gorgonzola cheese
4 thick pork chops
(10 -12 oz each),
with pockets
2 tbsps olive oil
salt and pepper to taste
oil for grill

Honey glazed thick straight sausages

Ingredients:

$4^1/_2$ lbs thick pork or
beef sausages
Honey and Chili
Marinade (page 124)
metal or bamboo
skewers

Method:

1 Smooth each sausage out straight and carefully push skewer through center end-to-end. Don't go off center or the sausage will curl. If using long metal skewers, thread 2 sausages.

2 Heat barbecue to normal for indirect heat and medium for direct heat. Grease the grill bars or hotplate and arrange sausages on the grill. Roll the sausages back and forth to gradually heat all sides evenly until there is a colour change. This gradually expands the skin and sausages will not burst.

3 Conyinue as follows:

Kettle or Hooded Barbecue – Place over indirect heat and brush with marinade. Cover with lid and cook for 20-25 minutes. Brush with marinade on all sides 3 more times during cooking. Remove skewers for final cooking.

Serves 4 to 8

Photograph page 38

Ingredients:

4 pork fillets (10 oz each)
³/₄ cup sun-dried tomato pesto
1 tbsp chopped basil
2 tbsps lemon juice
1 tbsp olive oil
1 quantity polenta (see page 75)

Piquant pork fillets with polenta

Method:

1   To make marinade, mix together sun-dried tomato pesto, chopped basil, lemon juice and olive oil.

2   Carefully remove the silvery white membrane from the top of the fillets with a sharp pointed knife. Place fillets in a suitable container and cover both sides with half of the marinade, (reserving remainder). Cover and marinate for 30 minutes at room temperature or longer in the refrigerator.

3   Cook as follows:

Charcoal Kettle or Hooded Gas Barbecue – Prepare barbecue for indirect cooking. Place the fillets on oiled grill bars over the drip tray. Cook with lid on for 40 minutes. Brush twice with some of the remaining marinade. When fillets are almost cooked, cut prepared polenta into 4x3in (10x7cm) slabs, remove from dish and brush with oil. Place over direct heat and cook for 4 minutes on each side until golden.

Flat-top and Electric Barbecue Grills – Heat until hot. Place a wire cake-rack to stand 1in (2.5cm) above grill bars. Place fillets on cake-rack and cook for approximately 20 minutes each side. Brushing with marinade when turned. Cut polenta as above and cook on oiled grill bars 5 minutes on each side.

To serve: Slice the fillets into 1in (2.5cm) thick diagonal slices. Overlap onto the polenta slice and top with the reserved and warmed marinade. Serve with suitable vegetables.

Serves 4   *Photograph also page 35*

Hawaiian pork kebabs

Method:

1   Place pork cubes in a non-metal container and stir in enough marinade to coat
    well. Cover and marinate for 30 minutes at room temperature, or longer in
    refrigerator.

2   Thread pork cubes onto skewers alternately with the pineapple, pepper and
    onion pieces. Brush with marinade and cook according to barbecue type.

Charcoal Kettle and Hooded Gas Barbecue – Prepare barbecue for indirect heat.
Place on oiled grill bars and brush well with marinade. Cook with lid or hood down
for 25-30 minutes, turn once or twice and brush with marinade.

Flat-top and Electric Barbecue Grill – Place a wire cake-rack to sit 1in (2.5cm)
over the grill bars. Heat barbecue until hot. Place the kebabs on grill and brush
with marinade. Turn after 5 minutes and brush again. Continue to cook for a total
time of approximately 25 minutes.

Serves 4–6

Loin of pork with sun-dried tomato and apple stuffing

Ingredients:

3¹/₄ lbs boned loin of pork
with flap on and rind removed
1 tbsp sun-dried tomato pesto
1 tbsp Honey and Chili Marinade
(page 124)

*Sun-dried Tomato
and Apple Stuffing*

1 cup soft white breadcrumbs
2 tablespoons sun-dried
tomato pesto
1 red apple, finely diced
1 tbsp Honey and Chili Marinade
(page 124)
salt, pepper

Method:

1 It is best to order the loin of pork, with the flap on, 2 days in advance as it is not usually included.

2 Score the fat layer in a diamond pattern with a pointed knife. Mix stuffing ingredients together and place along the roast, packing it up against the loin meat. Roll the flap over tightly; fasten with skewers while the roast is tied with kitchen string at 1in (2.5cm) intervals. Remove the skewers.

3 Rub the sun-dried tomato pesto over the surface of the rolled roast.

Cook as follows:

Kettle and Hooded Gas Barbecue – Prepare barbecue for indirect heat, normal or medium heat. Place the rolled loin over the drip pan, indirect heat, cover with lid or hood and cook for 50 minutes. Commence glazing with marinade every 10 minutes for a further 45-55 minutes; total cooking time is approximately 1¹/₄ to 1³/₄ hours. If using a meat thermometer, inside temperature should reach 167°-171°F (75°-77°C).

Electric Barbecue Grill with Hood – Set temperature to medium high or Hood range. Place roast in a foil pan and stand on a wire cake-rack to come 1in (2.5cm) above grill bars. Cover with hood and cook as above.

4 When cooked, wrap foil and stand 15 minutes before carving. Slice the roast and serve garnished with small Stuffed Apples (page 80) and vegetables of choice.

Serves 8 to 10   *Photograph page 45*

Ingredients:

8 center-cut pork chops 5 oz each
2 tbsps olive oil
6 tbsps Spice Rub for Meat
(see page 15)
oil for grill
Pico de Gallo
¼ cup minced onion
¼ cup minced green bell pepper
¼ cup minced red bell pepper
1 tsp minced garlic
1 bunch cilantro, minced
1 tbsp dried chillies, diced
½ cup fresh lime juice
½ cup white vinegar
salt and pepper to taste

Southwestern pork chops with pico de gallo

Method:

1   Lightly coat pork chops with olive oil. Massage chops with spice rub and let marinate at room temperature for at least 1 hour.

2   Prepare fire for direct-heat method of cooking (see page 13). A mesquite charcoal fire is recommended to give an authentic south-western flavor. When fire is ready, place meat on oiled grill. Cook chops on each side until golden brown, about 5 minutes per side. Chops should feel firm to the touch (145°F (63°C) on a meat thermometer). Serve with Pico de Gallo.

Note: Vast lonely mesas in the Southwest of America are covered with the scrubby mesquite tree. Long before trendy eateries discovered mesquite charcoal, locals did their barbecuing over mesquite logs. Serve the pork chops with warm, fresh corn tortillas and generous helpings of Pico de Gallo, a salsa perfumed with cilantro and lime.

Serves 4

Pork Chops with chili rice and glazed apples

Method:

1   Trim fat from chops as desired and sprinkle lightly with salt and pepper.

2   Heat barbecue until hot and oil the grill bars. Place the chops on grill and sear one side for one minute, turn and brush with Soy & Honey marinade to glaze. Continue to turn at 2 minute intervals 4 or 5 times more until cooked to required degree. Take care not to overcook. Cooking time is from 10-15 minutes depending on thickness of chops and type of barbecue used.

3   Place apple rings on the grill bars after the chops commence cooking. Turn 2-3 times until soft and glazed. Place a piece of parchment paper under the apples to prevent scorching. If cooking on a charcoal barbecue, use foil which has been brushed with oil.

4   Mix the chili and cooked rice together and heat on the side of the barbecue in a foil or metal dish. Serve chops with chili rice and garnish with glazed apple rings.

Serves 4-6

Ingredients:

6 pork loin chops about
$^1/_2$in (1.5cm) thick
salt and pepper
1 cup Soy and Honey Marinade
(page 124)
2 large apples, cored and
cut into thick rings
2 tsp chili powder
4 cups cooked rice

Warm Thai chicken salad

Ingredients:

3 chicken breasts
2 tsps Thai-style marinade (store bought)
1 tsp oil
1 red bell pepper, seeded and cut into strips
1 green bell pepper, seeded and cut into strips
1 eggplant, sliced
1 Spanish onion, cut into rings
1/2 head romaine lettuce, shredded
Dressing
1/2 cup olive oil
1/4 cup malt vinegar
1 tsp Thai-style marinade (store bought)

Method:

1 Flatten chicken breasts slightly to even thickness. Mix Thai-style marinade and oil together and rub well into the chicken. Cover and stand 20 minutes before cooking.

2 Heat the barbecue to medium-high and oil hotplate and grill bars. Place chicken on grill and cook 4 minutes each side. Place vegetables (except lettuce), on the hotplate, drizzle with a little oil and cook for 5-8 minutes, tossing and turning to cook through. Pile lettuce onto individual plates and place barbecued vegetables in the centre. Cut the chicken into thin diagonal slices and arrange over and around vegetables.

3 Mix dressing ingredients together and pour over chicken and warm salad. Serve with crusty bread.

Serves 3　　　　　　　　　　　　　　　*Photograph page 49*

Quick sesame chicken wings

Ingredients:

4 1/2 lbs chicken wings, tips removed
Soy and Honey Marinade (page 124)
3 tbsps sesame seeds, toasted

Method:

1 Place wings in a large container and smother with the marinade. Cover and marinate for 30 minutes at room temperature or longer in the refrigerator.

2 Place half the wings in a microwave-safe dish and microwave for 10 minutes on high. Remove and microwave the remainder.

3 Heat the barbecue until hot. Place a wire cake-rack over the grill bars and place the wings on the rack. Brush with marinade left in the bowl. Turn and brush the wings frequently until they are brown and crisp.

4 Spread sesame seeds on a foil tray and place on the barbecue. Shake occasionally as they toast. Sprinkle over the browned chicken wings. Serve as finger food.

Serves 4　　　　　　　　　　　　　　　*Photograph page 50*

Mustard and honey chicken drumsticks with mustard cream sauce

Ingredients:

4¹/₂ lbs chicken drumsticks
(medium-size)
1¹/₂ cups Honey and Chili
Marinade (page 124)
Mustard Cream Sauce
1¹/₄ cups sour cream
1 cup Dijon mustard
¹/₂ cup Honey and Chili Marinade
(page 124)

Method:

1 Place drumsticks in a non-metal container and pour enough marinade over to coat well. Cover and stand 30 minutes at room temperature or longer in the refrigerator.

2 To cook, prepare barbecue as follows:

Kettle and I looded Barbecues – Hcat until hot, place drumsticks over indirect heat and cover with lid or hood. Cook for 15 minutes. Remove hood, turn drumsticks and brush with marinade every 8 minutes, replacing hood until cooked (approximately 45 minutes cooking time). Continue turning and brushing with marinade as above 3 more times at 8 minute intervals or until drumsticks are cooked through to the bone. Total cooking time 60-65 minutes.

Flat-top, Charcoal and Gas Barbecues – Heat the barbecue until hot. Place a wire cake-rack over the grill bars and oil the rack. The rack should stand 1in (2.5cm) above the bars. Place the drumsticks on the rack and cook for 15-20 minutes, turning frequently. Place a square of parchment paper onto the grill bars. Transfer the drumsticks onto the parchment paper. Brush with marinade and turn frequently. Cook for a further 10-15 minutes until well glazed and cooked to the bone.

Mustard Cream Sauce: Mix the sour cream, mustard, honey & chili marinade together in a heat-proof bowl. Place at the side of the barbecue to heat through. Serve drumsticks with the mustard cream sauce and vegetable accompaniments or salad.

Serves 6/10   *Photograph page 56*

Cilantro swordfish steaks

Method:

1 Cream the butter until soft and mix in the cilantro and parmesan. Pile into butter pot and set aside.

2 Heat barbecue grill until hot and brush with oil. Brush fish steaks with oil, place on grill bars and cook 3-4 minutes each side according to thickness. Brush or spray vegetables with oil and place on grill, cook a few minutes on each side. Remove fish steaks and vegetables to heated plates. Top swordfish steak with a generous dollop of cilantro butter mixture and serve immediately.

Serves 4   *Photograph page 61*

Ingredients:

1/2 cup unsalted butter
2 tbsps cilantro, finely chopped
1 tbsp grated Parmesan cheese
4 swordfish steaks
1 tbsp olive oil
4 zucchini, cut into long slices
1 red bell pepper, quartered

Trout fillets

Method:

1 Mix the first 5 ingredients together in a shallow dish. Place the fillets in the dish and turn to coat well. Cover and stand 10-15 minutes.

2 Heat the barbecue to medium hot and oil the grill bars. Place a sheet of parchment paper over the bars and make a few slashes between the grill bars to allow ventilation. Place the fish on the paper and cook for 3-4 minutes each side according to thickness. Brush with marinade during cooking. Remove to plate. Heat any remaining marinade and pour over the fish.

3 Serve with baked potatoes and a salad.

Tip: Fish is cooked, if when tested with a fork, it flakes or the sections pull away.

Red Snapper, Haddock and Perch may also be used.

Serves 4

Ingredients:

1 tsp chopped fresh ginger
1 tsp crushed garlic
2 tbsps cilantro, finely chopped
2 tbsps olive oil
1 1/2 tbsps lemon juice
1 lb trout fillets
(4 portions)

Ginger salmon steaks with snowpeas and potato

Ingredients:

2 tsps chopped ginger
$1/2$ tsp chopped chili
2 tbsps oil
1 tbsp lime juice
2 tsps grated lime zest
4 salmon steaks
$1/2$ lb snowpeas, blanched
3 medium sized potatoes, parboiled in their jackets

Method:

1 Mix the ginger, chili, oil, lime juice and zest together. Pour half into a shallow dish or plate. Place salmon steaks in dish and pour over the remaining marinade. Stand 20 minutes before cooking.

2 Heat the flat-top or electric barbecue grill to medium-high and oil the grill bars. Cook salmon steaks 4 to 5 minutes each side, brushing with marinade as they cook. While cooking, place blanched snowpeas in foil and reheat on the barbecue. Slice the potatoes into $1/2$in (1cm) slices. Brush with oil and cook on the hotplate or grill bars a few minutes on each side. Serve immediately.

Serves 4   *Photograph page 65*

Sesame barbecued shrimp

Ingredients:

2 lbs medium-large jumbo shrimp
$1/4$ cup olive oil
$1/4$ cup red wine
4 shallots, finely chopped
1 tsp grated lemon zest
$1/2$ tsp cracked black peppercorns
12 bamboo skewers, soaked
$1/2$ cup sesame seeds

Method:

1 Peel and de-vein shrimp, leaving the shell tails intact.

2 Combine oil, wine, shallots, lemon zest and pepper. Mix well.

3 Thread the shrimp onto bamboo skewers (about 3 per skewer)

4 Place the skewers in a shallow dish and pour the marinade over. Allow to marinate in the refrigerator for a minimum of one hour.

5 Roll the shrimp in the toasted sesame seeds, pressing them on well. Refrigerate for about 30 minutes. Place on the barbecue and brush with marinade while grilling.

Serves 6

Grilled scallops with orange salsa

Ingredients:

2 small oranges
4 sun-dried tomatoes in oil,
drained and chopped
1 clove garlic, crushed
1 tbsp balsamic vinegar
4 tbsps extra virgin olive oil
salt and pepper
1 large head fennel, cut
lengthways into 8 slices
12 fresh prepared scallops
4 tbsps crème fraîche
arugula leaves to serve

Method:

1   Slice the top and bottom off 1 orange, then cut away
the peel and pith, following the curve of the fruit. Cut
between the membranes to release the segments,
then chop roughly. Squeeze the juice of the other orange
into a bowl, add the chopped orange, tomatoes, garlic,
vinegar and 3 tablespoons of the oil, then season with
salt and pepper.

2   Heat barbecue until hot and grease bars with oil.
Brush both sides of each fennel slice with half the
remaining oil. Cook for 2-3 minutes on each side,
until tender and charred. Transfer to serving plates
and keep warm.

3   Brush the scallops with the remaining oil and cook for 1
minute, then turn and cook for 30 seconds or until cooked
through. Top the fennel with 1 tablespoon of crème
fraîche, 3 scallops and the salsa. Serve with the
arugula.

Serves 4

Ingredients:

4 tuna steaks, about
6 oz each
1 tbsp olive oil
chopped fresh cilantro
to garnish
lime wedges to serve

For the salsa

3 ripe peaches, peeled,
stoned and finely chopped
4 green onions, finely chopped
¼ cup yellow bell pepper,
seeded and finely chopped
juice of ½ lime
1 tbsp chopped fresh cilantro
black pepper

Chargrilled tuna with peach salsa

Method:

1   First make the salsa. Place the peaches, green onions, pepper, lime juice, cilantro and black pepper in a small bowl and mix well. Cover and set aside for at least 1 hour to let the flavors mingle.

2   Preheat the grill to high. Brush the tuna with the oil and season with pepper. Grill for 3-5 minutes on each side, until the fish is cooked and the flesh is beginning to flake. Garnish with fresh cilantro and serve with the lime wedges and peach salsa.

Note: Fresh tuna, like other oil-rich fish, provides Omega 3 fatty acids which are important for a healthy heart. We should try to eat two portions of oil-rich fish a week.

Serves 4

Grilled salmon steaks with mint vinaigrette

Ingredients:

4 salmon steaks, about 6 oz each
salt and black pepper

For the vinaigrette
2 tbsps chopped fresh mint,
plus extra leaves to garnish
1 small shallot, finely chopped
6 tbsps olive or vegetable oil
juice of 1 lemon

Method:

1   Preheat the grill to high and line the grill tray with kitchen foil. Place the salmon steaks on top and season lightly. Grill for 4-5 minutes on each side until lightly browned and cooked through.

2   Meanwhile, make the vinaigrette. Mix together the mint, shallot, oil and lemon juice, then season to taste. Spoon over the salmon steaks and garnish with mint.

Note: This minty vinaigrette is very easy to make but it gives a new twist to salmon. You can also use the vinaigrette to dress a cucumber and potato salad to serve with it.

Serves 4

Cajun sea bass

Ingredients

6 thick fillets sea bass (8 oz each)
3 cloves garlic, ground
1/4 cup peanut oil
oil for grill

Cajun Black-Bean Sauce
6 cloves garlic, crushed
1 bunch green onions, sliced
1/4 cup peanut oil
1 cup dried shiitake mushrooms,
re-hydrated, drained and sliced
1 bunch cilantro, diced
5 slices fresh ginger
4 oz tasso, diced
4 oz fermented black beans, soaked and rinsed
1/2 cup Shaoxing or dry sherry
1/3 cup rice wine vinegar
1 cup chicken stock
1 tbsp cornstarch
1/4 cup cold water

1 Prepare fire for direct-heat method of cooking
   (see page 13).

2 Wash fish and pat dry. Rub fish with garlic and oil,
   cover and let rest at room temperature until time to
   begin cooking.

3 When Cajun Black-Bean Sauce is done and fire is
   ready, place fillets on oiled grill. Cook until fish is just
   done (3 to 4 minutes per side). Remove to warm
   serving platter and smother with sauce.

Serves 6

Cajun Black-Bean Sauce

1 In a large skillet on the stove, saute garlic and green
   onions in peanut oil until soft. Add drained mushrooms,
   cilantro, ginger, tasso and black beans. Saute until
   flavors meld together (about 5 minutes).

2 Add Shaoxing, vinegar and chicken stock to mixture.
   Reduce heat and simmer for 30 minutes.

3 In a small bowl mix cornstarch with the water and stir
   into vinegar-bean mixture. Simmer for 10 minutes more.
   Serve sauce over fillets.

*Note: Sea bass has a silky-smooth, meaty texture when
grilled. Imbued with the subtle smoky flavor of
mesquite, this fish is an excellent counterpoint to the
robust flavor of Cajun Black-Bean Sauce. If you can't
find tasso in your market, try substituting a smoky-
flavored bacon or Italian pancetta and add a touch of
cayenne pepper.*

Makes 2 cups

LET'S HAVE VEGETABLES ON THE GRILL

Vegetable Grill

Don't overlook vegetables when cooking on the grill. The simplest way to enjoy grilled vegetables is to cook them right along with a steak or chops. Slice zucchini and eggplant lengthwise 1/2in (1cm) thick and rub them down with minced garlic and olive oil and sprinkle them with fresh herbs. Place them on an oiled grill over direct heat.

When grilling vegetables as a side dish rather than as a main course, it is important to develop a sense of timing. Cooking three different things on a grill so that they are all done at the same time takes practice. Start by grilling one kind of vegetable by itself until you become comfortable. Time yourself so that you will know when to put the vegetable on the fire in conjunction with your main dish. Plan on using bigger fires since multiple dishes take up more grill space.

If you are adding vegetables to meat, poultry or seafood on skewers, cut the vegetables so that they will cook in the same amount of time as the meat or fish. An example is shrimp. You know that shrimp will cook quickly, so choose vegetables that will also cook quickly. Green onions, mushrooms and cherry tomatoes all cook as quickly as shrimp. If you want to add green bell peppers, onion, zucchini or other squashes, blanch them first to make up the difference in cooking time. Likewise, if you are using a meat that takes longer to cook, choose your vegetables accordingly.
For 1in (2.5cm) cubes of beef, try using raw pieces of red ball pepper, onion or zucchini. Whatever kind of vegetable you use, always lightly coat it with oil so that it will cook evenly.

Quick ratatouille

Ingredients:

2 medium-sized eggplant,
cut into ½ in (1cm) slices
4 zucchini, cut into
½ in (1cm) slices
1 large onion, cut in half & sliced
1 green bell pepper,
seeded & sliced
1 tsp crushed garlic
1¼ cup tomato salsa

Method:

1 Prepare vegetables. Oil a large foil tray and spread base with some of the salsa. Layer in the vegetables, spreading salsa between each layer. Cover with more salsa. Place over indirect heat in kettle of covered barbecue and cook for 30 minutes. For flattop barbecue, cover tray with foil, stand on a cake-rake placed over the grill bars and cook for 30 minutes.

Serves 4   *Photograph page 71*

Barbeque vegetable toss

Ingredients:

½ bunch shallots, trimmed
and cut into ¾ in (2cm) lengths
1 medium carrot, thinly sliced
1 cup cauliflower florets
1 cup snowpeas, trimmed
1 small sweet potato, thinly sliced
½ Chinese cabbage, roughly
chopped
1 cup Teriyaki Marinade
(page 124)

Method:

1 Heat the barbecue hotplate to medium high and oil well. Prepare vegetables and mix together. Pile onto the barbecue and spread out using tongs.

2 Place the cup of marinade in a metal container to heat through, which will make it flow more easily. Toss and cook the vegetables until they soften, then splash over the marinade while they complete cooking.

3 Remove to a pre-warmed serving dish while still a little crispy. Serve immediately with barbecued meats.

Note: Other vegetable combinations may be used according to preference.

Serves 2

Roasted garlic

When garlic is slowly roasted, the cloves steam inside their skins until creamy soft and deliciously sweet. Serve as an appetizer, squeezing the clove paste out of the skin and spreading over slices of baguette bread drizzled with the garlic juices. Brie cheese is an excellent complement. You might want to make this dish in conjunction with a slow-cooking roast because both require the indirect-heat method of cooking (see page 14).

6 medium heads garlic
¼ cup olive oil
4 tbsps unsalted butter
4 sprigs fresh oregano
1 baguette

1   Prepare fire for indirect-heat method of cooking (see page 14).

2   Cut the top end off the garlic heads, exposing the individual garlic cloves in their skins. Place the heads on one piece of heavy-duty aluminium foil and drizzle with olive oil. Dot with butter and lay oregano on top. Tightly seal aluminium foil to form a packet. Place on grill in a spot not directly over the coals.

3   After about 45 minutes, open packet (be careful of escaping steam) and baste heads with butter-oil mixture from bottom of packet. Reseal and continue to cook until garlic is spreadably soft (about 45 minutes more). Remove packet from grill and open carefully. Slice baguette into rounds, drizzle with butter-oil mixture from bottom of packet, squeeze softened garlic out of skins, and spread onto bread.

Serves 4-6

Fresh basil, tomato and cucumber salad

If you are a tomato gardener, consider growing basil as well. They both fare well in full sun or partial shade and prefer moderately rich soil that is kept lightly moist. If purchasing tomatoes, choose the very freshest, plumpest ripe ones that you can find. Allow this salad to marinate overnight. Don't add salt or pepper ahead of time. Let your guests season to their own taste. The flavors get more intense the longer they have to meld, making this an ideal choice for a picnic or any time you need a good make-ahead salad.

2 large cucumbers
4 large tomatoes
1 sweet red onion
½ bunch fresh basil
1½ to 2 cups distilled white vinegar

1   If cucumbers are waxed, peel them. If not, wash and score lengthwise with a fork around the circumference of cucumber to create an attractive design. Slice into quarter inch thick rounds.

2   Wash tomatoes and remove stems. Slice into quarter inch thick rounds.

3   Peel onion, slice into eighth inch rounds. Reserve. Stem basil, wash and pat dry. Chop half of the basil coarsely. Reserve remainder for garnish.

4   Arrange onions, tomatoes and cucumbers in serving bowl. Sprinkle with chopped basil and cover with vinegar. Cover and refrigerate at least 3 hours, preferably overnight. Before serving drain off most of the liquid. Garnish with remaining basil. Serve well chilled.

Serves 4-6

Pesto potato wedges

Method:

1   Peel and halve the potatoes, then cut each half into 4-6 wedges. Rinse well and drain, then place in a large bowl. Mix basil pesto, olive oil and water together. Pour over potatoes and toss to coat well. Place in a large foil dish in a single layer if possible and pour over any basil pesto mixture remaining in the bowl.

2   Cook over indirect heat in covered barbecue for 40 minutes, turning after 20 minutes. For flattop barbecue, cover with a sheet of foil and place foil tray on the hotplate. Cook 20 minutes then turn and cook 20 minutes more until tender.

3   When cooked, remove to a plate and sprinkle with Parmesan cheese.

Serves 4

Ingredients:

4 medium-sized potatoes
2 tbsps basil pesto
1 tbsp olive oil
1 tbsp water
¹/₂ cup grated Parmesan cheese

Grilled corn

This is a fun dish to make and very festive in presentation.

6 ears sweet corn, in husks.
oil for grill

1   Carefully peel husks away from corn but do not remove. Remove silk. Wash corn and husks.

2   Close husk around each ear and tie at the top with butcher's string. Place ears in large container of cold water to soak for at least 20 minutes.

3   Prepare fire for indirect-heat method of cooking (see page 14).

4   When fire is ready, squeeze out excess water from ears and lay them on oiled grill. Corn cooks by steaming inside husks. Turn ears occasionally. Corn is done when husks are evenly browned (15 to 20 minutes).

Serves 4 to 6

Polenta squares

If you are a fan of polenta, you may sometimes have the problem of what to do with your leftovers. This dish is so good that you may find yourself making polenta just so you can use "leftovers" to make this dish. Try substituting grits for polenta for your southern barbecues. Serve grilled polenta with an Italian mixed grill of sausages, chicken, eggplant, red peppers and zucchini with plenty of aioli and hot crusty French bread.

4 cups water
2 tsp salt
1 cup polenta
6 tbsps unsalted butter
1/2 cup grated Parmesan cheese
1/4 cup olive oil
oil for grill

1   In a large pot on the stove, bring the water and salt to a boil. Add polenta and stir constantly with a whisk until polenta begins to thicken. Transfer to a double boiler and slowly cook for 20 to 30 minutes, stirring occasionally, until thick and creamy. Whisk in butter and Parmesan cheese. Remove from heat and pour onto a 10x14 inch (25x35 cm) baking sheet, spreading polenta evenly with spatula until about 1-inch (2.5 cm) thick. Chill well in refrigerator (1 to 2 hours). If you are in a rush, quick-chill in the freezer (about 30 minutes).

2   Prepare fire for direct-heat method of cooking (see page 13). Cut polenta into 2 to 3-inch (5 to 7.5 cm) squares. Gently unmold from pan and lightly coat both sides with olive oil. When fire is ready, place squares on oiled grill and close lid. Flip over when one side is golden brown (about 5 minutes). Remove from fire when other side is golden brown (about 5 minutes more). Serve immediately.

Serves 6

Peppered pineapple

Ingredients:

1 small ripe pineapple, or 12 oz can
pineapple rings
1 tsp chopped chilli
1 tbsp brown sugar
1 tbsp melted butter

Method:

1 Combine the chopped chilli, brown sugar and melted butter
together.

2 Peel the pineapple. Cut into rings and remove the core.
Place on heated and oiled grill bars. Cook 1 minute on each
side then brush with chilli mixture and cook 2 minutes each
side. Serve with barbecued pork sausages, pork chops,
steaks or chicken.

Serves 4   *Photograph page 81*

Stuffed apples

Ingredients:

6 small, red crisp apples
2 cups fresh white breadcrumbs
1 small onion, very finely chopped
salt, pepper
1 tbsp raisins
2 tbsps Honey and Chili Marinade
(page 124)

Method:

1 Remove the core from the apples with a small, pointed knife.
Cut out more apple flesh to widen the hole. Chop the flesh
finely and add to the breadcrumbs. Mix in remaining ingredients
(except marinade). Pack the stuffing into the apples. Place
apples in a foil tray and brush over with honey & chili
marinade.

2 Place on barbecue using indirect heat or elevate on wire rack
over direct heat. Cover with lid or hood and cook for 30 minutes.
Serve as an accompaniment to roast pork or roast turkey.

Serves 6   *Photograph page 81*

Smoking Defined

Smoking is a food preparation process in which fat, water-soluble molecules, steam, and microscopic particles are released from burning wood and deposited on the surface of food placed in a smoker. The natural moisture in food absorbs the smoke flavors. Smoking also dries out the food. Drying concentrates the flavors and changes texture and appearance. By decreasing the moisture in food, smoking also helps to preserve it.

The smoking recipes in this chapter include those for cold smoking (a flavoring method but not a true cooking method) and for smoke cooking (a method which truly cooks food). Neither of these methods should be considered an adequate means of food preparation.

Cold Smoking

Cold smoking is the type of smoking common on plantations and country homes in the last two centuries. The term cold is misleading since it is by no means cold in the smokehouses. Cold smoking is "cold" only in the sense that it is done at cooler temperatures than smoke cooking. In general, cold smoking is done between 90°-130°F (32°-55°C). At these temperatures food is not cooked, although it may be dried by the process. Traditionally, highly salted meats were smoked in special houses or in the chimneys of large country fireplaces. They were smoked for days or even weeks, and although the temperature was insufficient to cook the food, the heavy smoke and high salt content discouraged the growth of bacteria, molds, and other fungi. Today this style of smoked food lives on as a flavoring method, most commonly used to produce country or "Virginia" hams, lox, some types of sausages, and bacon. Cold smoking can be done

successfully at home by using a kettle-shaped, covered water smoker as the recipes in this chapter for cold smoking illustrate. The recipes begin on page 94.

Smoke Cooking

Smoke cooking, also called hot smoking, refers to smoking at temperatures high enough to cook the food that is being smoked. Usually, smoke cooking is done at a temperature between 150°-250°F (66°-122°C). Smoke cooking at home has become quite popular since the advent of the kettle-shaped, covered water smoker. The recipes in this chapter for smoke cooking were designed to use this type of water smoker. More information on this equipment is provided on page 114. Smoke cooking recipes begin on page 96.

Smoking Equipment

Gas or electric smokers are small versions of the type of smoker used commercially. All smokers consist of a metal box with a heating element on the bottom. A pan holds smoldering wood chips or hardwood sawdust over the element. Food is held on a rack or suspended on hooks. By paying careful attention to temperature and heat source, you can use these smokers for both cold smoking and smoke cooking. If you want to try cold smoking, follow the instructions for cold smoking as adapted for the water smoker (see page 93). If you want to smoke cook, follow the basic guidelines presented on the opposite page and the manufacturer's instructions provided with your smoker. Gas and electric smokers were not tested for this book. Instead, all recipes were tested using a kettle-shaped, covered water smoker. However, these recipes can be adapted for gas and electric smokers. Consult your instruction manual for details.

Homemade Smokers

These may be as simple as an oil drum, a garbage
can, or an old refrigerator. Or they may be as elaborate
as a brick smokehouse. Like the commercial variety,
homemade smokers consist of a heat source (such as
a hot plate), a pan to hold chips or sawdust, and racks
or poles from which to suspend the food.

These smokers are particularly suitable for cold
smoking, but using them for smoke cooking can
sometimes be difficult because consistent high
temperatures cannot be maintained. You may prefer to
smoke the food first and then finish the cooking in a
kitchen oven set to 200°-250°F (90°-120°C). These
types of smokers were not tested for use with the
recipes in this book.

Pork butt bacon

Ingredients:

2 pork butts (5^1/$_2$ - 6^1/$_2$ lbs each)
1 recipe Basic Brine, with sodium
nitrite (see page 115)

Method:

1   Pork butt makes a lean and delicious bacon. These chunks can also
be roasted whole with a sweet sugar or honey glaze, just like ham.
Once roasted, the bacon can be eaten hot or cold. This pork is not
fully cooked after the smoking process; it must be cooked before it
can be eaten. Either slice and fry as you would bacon or roast
whole to an internal temperature of 155°-165°F (68°-74°C).

2   Have a butcher remove bone from pork butts. Cut each butt into
4 to 6 large chunks of approximately equal size. Prepare brine.
Place meat into a non aluminum container. Cover with brine.
Weight down meat with a heavy plate so that the pieces stay
submerged. Refrigerate for 1 to 2 days. To test if meat is completely
cured, cut a chunk in half and check color. Cured meat is uniformly
pink all the way through.

3   Remove meat from brine and discard brine. Wash meat and pat
dry. Place meat on a wire rack (such as a cake rack) or tie with string
and suspend from a pole and use an electric fan to circulate air
around meat. Let meat dry until surface is dry to the touch (16 to 24
hours).

Prepare water smoker for cold smoking (see page 93). Place meat
on grill. Cover and smoke at no greater than 130°F (54°C) for at least
6 hours or overnight. Periodically stir sawdust and add more as
needed. Remove meat from smoker. Cool to room temperature
before refrigerating. Well wrapped Pork Butt Bacon will keep 1 to 2
weeks refrigerated or up to 2 months in the freezer.

Makes 8-10 lbs (4-5kg) bacon

Smoked pork loin (Canadian bacon)

Method:

Ingredients:

*2 boneless center cut
pork loin (4¹/₃ - 6¹/₂ lbs each)
1 recipe Basic Brine
(see page 115)*

1 Smoked pork loin is left whole and prepared in exactly the same way as Pork Butt Bacon (see page 89). Depending on the thickness of the loin, it will require 3 to 5 days to cure. Follow all instructions for Pork Butt Bacon. If curing for more than 3 days, don't forget to overhaul the cure (see page 112 for instructions).

Once smoked the pork is not fully cooked but can be roasted to an internal temperature of 150°F (66°C), or sliced and fried as Canadian bacon. Roasted pork loins are also good served cold in sandwiches.

Makes 7-10 lbs (3.5-5kg) pork loin

Country style dry cured bacon

Ingredients:

*1 whole pork belly (9-11 lbs)
1 recipe Basic Dry Cure
(see page 103)*

Method:

1 Trim pork belly so edges are square. Cut belly in half so that it fits on the smoker. Rub about half the dry cure mixture into all sides and edges of both pieces of meat and reserve remaining mixture. Place pieces into a heavy duty plastic bag, one skin-side down and the other on top of it so the skin side is up. Seal the bag and place into a pan large enough to hold the belly pieces. Refrigerate for a total of 4 days. After 1 or 2 days, meat juices and dry cure form a natural brine. Turn the bag over each day. After the fourth day remove belly pieces, discard liquid and rub meat with reserved dry cure. Return belly to the plastic bag and continue to cure another 4 to 6 days, turning the bag over each day.

2 Remove meat from the plastic bag. Wash and pat dry. Place meat on a wire rack (such as a cake rack) or tie with string and suspend meat from a pole in front of an electric fan so that air circulates around it. Let meat dry until surface is no longer tacky to the touch (16 to 24 hours).

3 Prepare water smoker for cold smoking (see page 91). Place meat into smoker, skin side down on the grill. Cover and smoke at no higher than 120°F (49°C) for at least 6 hours and up to 24 hours. Periodically stir sawdust and add more as needed.

4 Remove bacon, let cool to room temperature and wrap before refrigerating. Well wrapped, refrigerated bacon will keep for 2 to 3 weeks.

Makes 6-8 lbs (3-4kg) bacon

Step by Step for Smoke Cooking

Recipes in this book for smoke cooking (also called hot smoking) were designed for use with a kettle shaped, covered, home-style water smoker. Consult the chart on page 121 to determine how many charcoal briquettes and how much wood to use and the cooking time for each type of food. All smoke cooking must be done outside, out of reach of children and pets. Be careful of wind, which may blow the smoke into your house – or worse – your neighbor's.

1 Set up water smoker outside. Remove the top and center ring and open all vents. Start charcoal briquettes in a charcoal chimney, or place them directly on bottom grill inside ring and start with an electric starter. Coals are ready when coated with a light gray ash (about 30 minutes). Spread coals evenly across the inside of the charcoal ring. Place water pan in position and fill with desired hot liquid. Set lower grill over water pan. Carefully set middle ring in place on top of the bottom section.

2 Soak 2x3in (5x8cm) wood chunks of choice in water for at least 1 hour. Shake off excess water. Open side door and, using tongs, place wood on top of coals. Consult the chart on page 121, and start with the least amount of wood recommended.

Preparation of food for smoke cooking varies with the recipe. Some foods need to be coated with spices or a marinade; others are brushed with oil before being placed in the water smoker. Set cooking racks in place and add food in a single layer. Leave about 1-2in (2.5-5cm) between pieces of food so smoke can circulate. If cooking different foods with varying cooking times, place the food that will be done first on the top racks. Remember that foods above will drip on foods below, so do not allow foods to drip if the flavors are incompatible.

Partially close all vents while smoke cooking. Use oven mitts or hot pads when adjusting vents. Insert instant-read thermometer into top vent. After 30 minutes the thermometer should read at least 170°F (77°C). The ideal range is between 170°-250°F (77°C-122°C).

Remember: The water smoker functions best when not nursed.

3 Try not to pen the lid of the water smoker while you're cooking. After 3½ to 4 hours, you will probably need to add more hot water to the water pan. The pan should always be at least half full. For longer periods of smoking, you will need to add more briquettes and possibly more wood. Add a dozen or so briquettes every 1½ hours.

If the smoker is not maintaining sufficient heat (at least 170°F (77°C), open the vents. If the fire is dying out, open the front door of the smoker. The additional oxygen will get the fire going again. If the smoker is still too cool, add more briquettes.

If the temperature is too hot (above 250°F(122°C)), try closing the vents more. If this doesn't work, add some cold water to the water pan or remove some of the briquettes.

4 Smoke cooked meat is often pink below the outer surface, so rely on temperature. See the individual recipes for a rough guide to internal temperatures of cooked meat. Insert the thermometer into the thickest part of the food, making sure it does not touch bone.

Smoke Cooking

Smoke cooking, also called hot smoking, refers to smoking at temperatures high enough to cook the food that is being smoked. Usually, smoke cooking is done at a temperature between 150°F-250°F (66°-122°C). Smoke cooking at home has become quite popular since the advent of the kettle-shaped, covered water smoker.

The recipes in this chapter for smoke cooking were designed to use this type of water smoker. More information on this equipment is provided on page 103. Smoke cooking recipes begin on page 95.

Smoked beef brisket with barbecue sauce

Ingredients:

1 beef brisket (9 lbs)
3 cloves garlic, minced
1 tbsp salt
1 tsp black pepper
2 tsps paprika
1/2 tsp each cayenne pepper, dried thyme and ground cumin
1 tsp dried mustard
2 cups barbecue sauce

Barbecue Sauce
1/2 cup vegetable oil
1 onion, finely chopped
1/2 green bell pepper, finely chopped
2 tsps ground garlic
2 cups ketchup
1/2 cup molasses
2 tsps hot sauce, such as Tabasco Sauce™
1/4 cup medium hot mustard
2 tbsps cider vinegar
1/2 cup dark brown sugar
4 tbsps Worcestershire sauce
1 tsp smoke flavoring
1/2 cup fresh lemon juice

Method:

1 The water smoker must have been invented to cook briskets. This tough cut of meat comes out juicy and tender with a wonderful smoky flavor. Leftover brisket can be rewarmed by slicing and simmering in your favorite tomato based barbecue sauce (see page 122-3) over low heat for 10 minutes.

2 Wash brisket. Trim away large chunks of fat, leaving at least a 1/4 in (5 cm) thick layer of fat. Rub garlic and salt all over brisket. Combine black pepper, paprika, cayenne, thyme, cumin and mustard; rub mixture over brisket to coat meat. Cover with plastic wrap and let rest at room temperature for 1 to 3 hours.

3 Prepare water smoker for smoke cooking (see page 102). Place brisket, fat side up, on the grill. Cover and smoke cook at a temperature between 200°-250° (93°-122°C) . Add charcoal briquettes, wood and water as needed. Brisket is done when internal temperature reaches 160°-170°F (71°-77°C) (after 5 to 8 hours of cooking).

4 Remove meat to a large platter or cutting board. Let rest 15 minutes before slicing. Serve with heated barbecue sauce.

Serves 6 to 8

Barbecue sauce

Method:

1 Place oil in a large non-aluminium saucepan, then saute onion, green pepper and garlic until soft (about 10 minutes). Add remaining ingredients and continue to simmer slowly for 20-30 minutes. Stir frequently to prevent sauce from burning. Let rest for at least one hour after cooking to allow the flavors to meld.

Makes about 4 cups

Ingredients:

2 chickens (3¹/₄ lbs each)
1 gallon water
1¹/₄ lbs salt
²/₃ cup sugar
³/₄ cup soy sauce
1 tsp each dried tarragon,
dried thyme and pepper
¹/₄ cup olive oil

Smoked chicken

Method:

1 Thoroughly wash birds inside and out. Put the water in a large non-aluminum container and in it dissolve salt and sugar. Add soy sauce, tarragon, thyme and pepper. Submerge birds in the brine and weight them down with a heavy plate so they stay submerged. Marinate in refrigerator overnight or at room temperature for 2 hours.

2 Remove birds from brine, wash and pat dry. Reserve brine. Truss birds for cooking.

3 Prepare water smoker for smoke cooking (see page 100). Fill water pan with hot water and half the reserved brine. Place birds, breast side up on the grill. Cover and smoke cook at 200°-250°F (93°-122°C). Add charcoal briquettes, wood and water as needed. Brush birds with olive oil every 2 hours. Chickens are done when internal temperature of the thickest part of the thigh registers 160°-170°F (71°-77°C), about 4 hours of cooking time. Remove birds from smoker and let rest 10 minutes. Carve and serve. Well wrapped leftovers will keep 3 to 5 days refrigerated.

Note: It is always a good idea to make more than one bird when using this recipe since there is little additional work involved. You can eat the extra chicken cold (which is just as delicious as the hot version), and use the smoked meat in other dishes such as salads or sandwiches.

Serves 8

Smoked duck

Ingredients:

2 ducks (4¹/₂ - 6³/₄ lbs each)
1 recipe Chinese brine for
duck or chicken (see page 106)
1 tsp Chinese five-spice powder
1 ginger root (about ¹/₄ lb), sliced
into ¹/₄ inch thick slices
6 whole star anise,
soaked in water for at least
30 minutes

Method:

1 Wash ducks thoroughly inside and out. Place ducks in a large non-aluminum container, cover with brine and weight birds down with a heavy plate so that they stay submerged. Refrigerate 16 to 20 hours. Remove from brine and reserve brine. Wash ducks and pat dry. Sprinkle cavity of each with five-spice powder. Truss ducks.

2 Prepare water smoker for smoke cooking (see page 100). Put 2 cups reserved brine in the pan, then fill pan with hot water. Place ducks breast side up on the grill. Cover and smoke cook at temperature between 200°-250°F (93°-122°C).

3 Add charcoal briquettes, wood and water as needed. Check the internal temperature of ducks after about 3 hours. When it reaches 150°F (66°C), add the ginger root and star anise to the coals. The duck is done when the internal temperature of the meat registers 155°-165°F (68°-74°C) (about 4 hours of cooking). Remove ducks from smoker. Let rest 10 minutes before cutting into quarters with poultry shears and serving.

Note: The Chinese are the masters of duck cookery. This recipe combines Chinese spicing and flavors with smoke cooking for a fragrant, succulent result.

The cooking temperature given in this recipe will probably produce a slightly less than well done duck. If you like well done duck, smoke to an internal temperature of 170°-175°F (77°-80°C).

Each duck serves 4

Smoked trout

Ingredients:

6 to 8 whole trout, gutted
(13-26 oz each)
1 recipe Fish brine (see page 116)
1/2 cup vegetable oil

Method:

1   Place fish in a non-aluminum container. Cover with brine. Place a heavy plate on fish so that they remain submerged. Let rest 45 minutes to 1½ hours, depending on the size of fish and the saltiness you desire. (Experiment and keep notes.) Remove fish from brine, wash and pat dry.

2   Prepare water smoker for smoke cooking (see page 100). Don't use the water pan. Ideally, the smoker temperature should be maintained between 150°-190°F (66°-88°C). Brush fish lightly with oil and place on grill. Cover and smoke cook until flesh can just be flaked with a fork, 45 minutes to 1½ hours of cooking. Remove fish from grill and brush with additional oil. Fish can be eaten immediately or allowed to cool to room temperature. If cooked, wrap well and refrigerate or freeze until use.

Note: Trout is a fish that takes well to smoke. If you or someone you know is successful at fishing, you may have more trout than you know what to do with. Smoking not only increases the length of time you can keep the trout, but smoked trout can also be frozen. Once smoked, trout will keep refrigerated for 5 to 7 days; smoked and frozen, it will keep for 2 to 3 months. This recipe works well for any small 12-24oz (340-680g) whole fish, including mackerel, whitefish and bluefish. Although the fish can be eaten hot, it is especially good cold as an appetizer or light lunch.

Serves 6 to 8

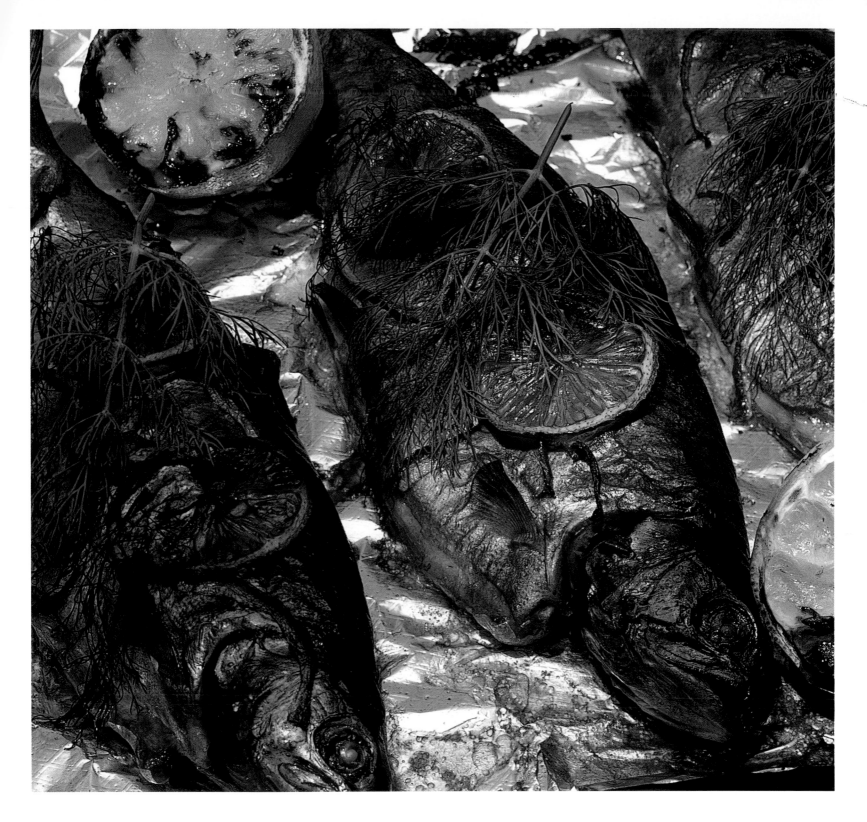

Cooking in brine

The brining of meat and fish before smoking provides the salty flavor characteristic of many smoked foods. Brine, also called wet cure or pickle, is a solution of salt, water, sugar, and – often – sodium nitrite. Meat placed in a brine solution cures by having its moisture content reduced and the moisture replaced with salt. The addition of sodium nitrite to the brine not only gives the meat the traditional pink color but retards the growth of botulism.

Nitrite need be present in cures only if the meat will be subject to prolonged cold smoking (longer than 3 to 4 hours). During cold smoking the temperature is ideal for bacterial growth. Nitrite does not need to be used for meat that will be smoke cooked since the temperature is high enough to cook the food before bacterial growth can occur. Spices and other flavoring can be added to the brine for additional flavor.

Sodium nitrite

The United States Department of Agriculture, which oversees the commercial processing of meat, requires that only 1/4 oz (6.1g) of sodium nitrite be used to cure 100 pounds of meat.

When smoking small batches of meat at home, the proportionate amount of sodium nitrite is so small that it is difficult to measure accurately. As a result, the home cook usually buys a commercial preparation in which sodium nitrite has been cut with other substances such as salt and dextrose. Figure that instead of 1/4 oz (6.1g), 4 oz (115g)of this sodium mixture is used to cure 100 pounds of meat.

These curing salts are sold under brand names like Prague Powder and Ham Cure, and the products can be purchased from butcher supply houses.

Curing times

Many variables affect the timing of the curing process. The three most important are the strength of the cure (how salty it is), the temperature during curing and the thickness of the piece of meat to be cured. In commercial operations needles are inserted into large pieces of meat and brine is pumped under pressure through the needles into the meat. This speeds curing and aids in the distribution of the cure. Most home cooks do not have injection needles and pumps, however, and must rely on the old fashioned method of passive diffusion. Passive diffusion works fine for smaller cuts of meat. The curing of large pieces of meat, such as whole hams, is beyond the scope of this book.

The curing times given in the individual recipes are only guidelines. Keep records of results in a journal, and adjust the timing of subsequent efforts to suit your taste. If the meat is too salty, decrease the curing time. If not salty enough, increase the curing time.

Remember: If curing takes longer then 2 hours, do it in the refrigerator.

Basic brine

Ingredients:

1 gallon water
1½ cups kosher salt
1 cup sugar (granulated or firmly packed brown)
½ cup curing salt
(sodium nitrite mixture)

Method:

1   Place the water in a 2 gallon (7 litre) non-aluminum, non-cast iron container. Add salt and sugar, stirring continuously until completely dissolved. Add curing salt and stir until dissolved. Submerge meat in liquid and place a heavy plate on top to keep it completely submerged. If meat is to be cured for more than 3 days, overhaul brine. To do this, remove meat. Stir brine, making sure that undissolved particles dissolve. Replace meat and weigh down with a heavy plate.

Note: This recipe is good for bacon, pork loins and hams. Follow these steps for the other brine recipes that do not list instructions as well.

Corned beef or pastrami brine

Ingredients:

1 gallon water
2 cups kosher salt
1 cup sugar
$^1/_4$ cup pickling spice
1 tbsp granulated garlic
2 tbsps cracked peppercorns
8 bay leaves
$^1/_2$ cup curing salt (sodium nitrite),
optional

Meat

2 trimmed beef briskets $6^1/_3$-$8^1/_2$
lbs each or 4 beef plates $3^1/_2$-$4^1/_2$
lbs each
2 cups cracked cilantro seed
1 cup cracked peppercorns

Method:

1   In a 2 gallon (7 litre) non-aluminum pot, combine the water, salt, sugar, pickling spice, garlic, peppercorns, bay leaves and curing salt (if used). Bring to a boil and stir until salts and sugar are dissolved. Cover pot and reduce heat to a simmer. Cook 20 minutes. Remove from heat and cool to room temperature. Refrigerate until cold, about 2 hours.

2   Place meat in a non-aluminium container and cover with brine. Weigh down meat with a heavy plate so that it stays submerged. Place container in refrigerator and cure for 3-4 days. At this point overhaul brine (see page 113). Continue to cure for another 3-4 days or until cure has penetrated to the center of meat. Remove meat, wash and drain. Combine cilantro and pepper and rub all over meat.

3   Prepare water smoker for smoke cooking (see page 100). Use only 30 briquettes to begin so that the smoker does not exceed 200°F (93°C). Use 5 to 8 wood chunks. Place meat on both racks of smoker, cover, and smoke cook until internal temperature of meat is 120°-130°F (49°-54°C), about 3-4 hours cooking time.

4   Add enough briquettes (about 40) and 2-3 chunks wood or three cups wood chips to the fire to build up the temperature in the smoker to between 220°-250°F (104°-122°C). Continue to smoke cook until the internal temperature of meat is 160°-165°F (71°-74°C), another 3 to 4 hours cooking time. Remove meat and let rest 10 minutes before slicing. Refrigerate leftovers.

Note: The brine for pastrami must be cooked to bring out the flavor of the pickling spice..

Each brisket makes enough for 15 sandwiches; each plate makes enough for 10 sandwiches

Chinese brine for duck or chicken

Ingredients

1 gallon water
1¹/₂ cups kosher salt
1 cup sugar
¹/₂ cup light soy sauce
1 tsp Chinese five spice powder
2 slices fresh ginger

Fish brine

Ingredients

1 gallon water
1¹/₂ cups kosher salt
¹/₂ cup soy sauce
1 cup sugar
2 bay leaves
1 tsp dried dill or 4 sprigs fresh dill
zest of 2 lemons

Spicy brine for beef, lamb, pork or veal

Ingredients

1 gallon water
1¹/₂ cups kosher salt
1 cup sugar
2 tsps cayenne pepper
2 tbsps pepper
2 tbsps cumin seed
1 tsp whole thyme, oregano or basil leaves
1 tbsp garlic, ground

Lamb and venison brine

Ingredients

1 gallon water
1¹/₄ cups kosher salt
¹/₂ cup soy sauce
1 cup sugar
2 tbsps mustard seed
6 whole allspice berries, crushed
1 tbsp dried summer savory
2 tbsps ground garlic

Basic dry cure

Ingredients

2 cups kosher salt
1 cup firmly packed brown sugar
1/4 cup curing salt (sodium nitrite mixture)
4 tbsps black pepper

Fish dry cure

Ingredients

2 cups kosher salt
1/4 cup sugar
1 tbsp pepper
1 tsp dried dill
1 tsp dried oregano

... and dry cures

A dry cure is a mixture of salt, sugar and, sometimes, sodium nitrite that is rubbed directly on meat or fish.

It is the traditional method used to cure country hams and bacon. You may find it difficult to control the saltiness of the final product, especially on larger cuts of meat such as hams. For home use, the dry cure method is most suitable for smaller pieces of food, such as fish fillets and pork bellies.

All dry cures are made in the same manner. In a small plastic container, combine ingredients. Cover and shake to mix.

Cooking chart for water smokers

	Weight or Thickness	Charcoal	Cooking Time*	Number of Wood Chunks	Types of Wood**	Internal Temperature When Done***
Beef						
Boneless roasts	3-6 lbs	2 layers	4-6 hours	4-6	H, M, C, O, GV	125°F (52°C) rare 140°F (60°C) medium
Brisket of beef	6-8 lbs	2 layers	5-7 hours	5-8	H, M, C, O, GV	160°-170°F (71°-77°C) well
Short ribs	2-3in (5-7.5cm)	2 layers	3-4 hours	4-6	H, M, C, O, GV	160°-170°F (71°-77°C) well
Prime rib bones	1/2in each(1.5cm)	1 layer	2-3 hours	3-5	H, M, C, O, GV	140°F (60°C) medium
Lamb and game						
Leg of lamb	5-7 lbs	2 layers	4-6 hours	4-6	H, C, O, AP	140°-160°F (60°-71°C) medium
Venison roast	5-7 lbs	2 layers	4-6 hours	4-6	H, C, O, AP	160°-170°F (71°-77°C) well
Lamb shanks	1 lb each	2 layers	3-4 hours	4-6	H, C, O, AP	160°-170°F (71°-77°C) well
Lamb chops	1-1½in thick (2.5-40cm)	1 layer	2-3 hours	4-6	H, C, O, AP	130°-140°F (54°-60°C) medium
Pork						
Boneless pork butt	4-6 lbs	2 layers	4-6 hours	5-8	H, AP, C, AL, GV, M	160°-170°F (71°-77°C) well
Boneless pork loin	3-5 lbs	2 layers	3-5 hours	4-6	H, AP, C, AL, GV, M	150°-160°F (66°-71°C) well
Fresh leg	12-18 lbs	2 layers	8-12 hours	7-10	H, AP, C, AL, GV, M	160°-170°F (71°-77°C) well
Pork chops	1¼in (3cm)	2 layers	2-3 hours	4-6	H, AP, C, AL, GV, M	150°-160°F (66°-71°C) well
Ribs	Full slab	2 layers	3-5 hours	4-6	H, AP, C, AL, GV, M	160°-170°F (71°-77°C) well
Ham (cooked)	10-14 lbs	2 layers	3-4 hours	2-4	H, AP, C, AL, GV, M	130°F (54°C)
Pork sausage (raw)	1in (.5cm) thick, such as Italian	1 layer	1½-2½ hours	2-4	H, AP, C, AL, GV, M	150°-160°F (66°-71°C) well
Fish						
Whole, small	3/4-1½ lbs	½ layer	3/4-1½ hours	2-4	AL, GV, O, M, H	Flakes
Whole, large	3-6 lbs	1 layer	3-4 hours	4-6	AL, GV, O, M, H	Flakes
Steak, fillet	1-1½in (2.5-3.5cm)	1 layer	1-2½ hours	2-4	AL, GV, O, M, H	Flakes
Shellfish		1 layer	½-1½ hours	2-4	AL, GV, O, M, H	Firm to touch

Cooking chart for water smokers

	Weight or Thickness	Charcoal	Cooking Time*	Number of Wood Chunks	Types of Wood**	Internal Temperature When Done***
Poultry						
Chicken	Cut up	1 layer	3-4 hours	2-4	AP, AL, C, GV, M, H, O	160°-170°F (71°-77°C) juicy
	3½-4½ lbs	2 layers	4-5 hours	3-5	AP, AL, C, GV, M, H, O	160°-170°F (71°-77°C) juicy
	5 lbs	2 layers	5-6 hours	4-6	AP, AL, C, GV, M, H, O	155°-165°F (68°-74°C) juicy
Turkey (unstuffed)	8-12 lbs	2 layers	7-8 hours	6-8	AP, AL, C, GV, M, H, O	160°-170°F (71°-77°C) juicy
	13-18 lbs	2 layers	9-12 hours	7-10	AP, AL, C, GV, M, H, O	160°-170°F (71°-77°C) juicy
Duck	4-6 lbs	2 layers	4-6 hours	3-5	AP, AL, C, GV, M, H, O	155°-165°F (68°-74°C) juicy
Cornish game hen	1-1½ lbs	1 layer	2-4 hours	2-4	AP, AL, C, GV, M, H, O	160°-170°F (71°-77°C)
Small birds	¾-1½ lbs	1 layer	2-4 hours	2-4	AP, AL, C, GV, M, H, O	160°-170°F (71°-77°C)
Pheasant	2-3 lbs	2 layers	3-5 hours	3-5	AP, AL, C, GV, M, H, O	160°-170°F (71°-77°C)
Vegetables						
Winter squash (butternut, banana, acorn)	¾-1in (2-2.5cm)	2 layers	2-3 hours	2-4	H, AP, C	Knife inserts easily
Summer squash (zucchini, crookneck, pattypan, golden zucchini)	Medium size	2 layers	1-2 hours	2-4	H, AP, C, M	Tender and soft
Onion	Medium	2 layers	2½-3½ hours	2-4	H, AP, C, M	Soft
Bell pepper	Medium	2 layers	¾-1½ hours	2-4	H, AP, C, M	Soft
Tomato	Medium	2 layers	½-¾ hours	2-4	H, AP, C, M	Soft
Corn	Whole	2 layers	½-¾ hours	2-4	H, AP, C, M	Tender
Garlic	Whole head	2 layers	2-3 hours	2-4	H, AP, C, M	Soft
Eggplant	½ in (1.5cm) slices	2 layers	1½-2½ hours	2-4	H, AP, C, M	Soft

*The cooking times used in this chart are for meat that has been completely thawed. If frozen foods are used they should be completely defrosted. Always allow an extra 30 minutes of cooking–it is better to allow too much time rather than too little time. Foods can be kept hot beyond recommended time as long as the water pan is more than half full.

**AL = Alder, AP = Apple, C = Cherry, GV = Grapevine, H = Hickory, M = Mesquite, O = Oak.

***Insert instant-read thermometer into thickest part of meat or poultry. It should not touch bone.

Campfire Cooking

Cooking over a campfire, a part of everyday life just a few generations ago, can throw the most experienced modern cook off stride. Faced with the unfamiliar tasks of gathering wood and turning out a full meal over a smoky fire, campfire cooks could possibly forget that camping is supposed to be fun. The first rule of campfire cooking is to do as much pre-trip preparation as possible. Learning to cook over a fire can take some practice, so start with basic recipes – everyone knows that even simple foods taste great out of doors. Recipes in this chapter are easy yet so elegant that your camping companions may forget that they're supposed to be roughing it.

Campfire Cooking Takes Planning

Paying attention to details ahead of time will make your camp cooking – and your whole camping experience – easier and more fun. Your camping style is, of course, the major factor in the type of campfire cooking you'll be doing, the amount of food you'll bring, and how you'll need to pack it. Hikers and backpackers must be constantly aware of weight and bulk when planning menus and packing food and equipment. Campground campers or "car campers" have fewer restrictions but should try and minimize the number of items.

When packing for camping have on hand sealable plastic bags (both quart and gallon sizes), a ballpoint or indelible marking pen (other types may smear and become illegible if they get wet), and a roll of self-adhesive labels for identifying the food and the meal it's for. Include cooking instructions on the label if necessary. If you label all containers, you won't have to open them until it's time to use those ingredients. Pre-written instructions will help you to stay organized and allow you to delegate some cooking jobs in camp.

Take foods that don't take up much room – especially valuable cooler space. You can shop at outdoor equipment stores for backpacking food that doesn't need refrigeration. Some types of freeze-dried foods leave much to be desired, but some are fine; experiment with different brands before you take them on the road. If plenty of water will be available at your camp site, consider bringing powdered juice mixes instead of large containers of drinks. If you will be away from refrigeration, take along powdered milk to supplement your milk supply.

Because space is a concern, it's a good idea to repackage some food. Transfer bulk food to containers that are smaller, more efficient, unbreakable, and leak proof. Remember to always label anything you repackage. The plastic containers that film is sold in are useful for carrying spices, fresh herbs, and small, loose items such as matches.

Outdoor equipment stores and mail order firms carry backpacking supplies that can help you pack food efficiently. Look for plastic food tubes that can be filled and sealed from the bottom. These are good for transporting peanut butter, mustard, honey, and jams. They are especially helpful on a day hike where you'll be preparing lunch away from camp.

Plastic bottles especially designed for camping come in all sizes and are wonderful for carrying liquids because they don't leak after you give the lid an extra twist. Keep in mind that oils are likely to leak so give the lid of oil containers an extra twist, then enclose the entire bottle in a sealable plastic bag for extra insurance.

The best way to carry eggs is to break them into a plastic bottle (leave yolks whole and unbeaten until you're ready to use them). By breaking them beforehand you avoid having messy broken eggs in the camp cooler.

When planning preparation at home, begin by laying out a chart with the number of days and the meals to be served each day, and then list the foods to take along.

When planning menus always think about ease of preparation in camp. Prepare one pot meals in your home kitchen, seal them into a plastic container, and simply heat them in a pot on the campfire for dinner the first night. Wash and cut all vegetables and salad ingredients at home, and store them in plastic bags in your camp cooler until needed.

Mix dry ingredients for recipes such as Polenta Squares (see page 75) at home, and put the mix into a bag.

Don't forget to label all bags and to include instructions about use and preparation. A well organized packing job will spare you the frustration of continually searching for things in camp.

Keeping a permanent checklist of your camping supplies, utensils, and gear can save you hours of work before a trip. If you do a lot of camping, you may want to buy a portable cupboard from one of the companies that supplies camping equipment for outfitters and in it keep a permanent "kitchen" complete with basic staples, spices, and cooking utensils. If you don't want to go to that expense, several heavy-cardboard boxes with lids and handholds (such as those for storing business files) will do a fine job of organizing. Use a bold marking pen to label the boxes on the top and on all sides.

It's a good idea to pack together things you use at the same time. Think about the things you'll need when you first arrive in camp, for example, water containers and the equipment to get your campfire going. Pack those items together and put that box on top in your trunk. Use logic: first used, last packed.

If you are car camping for several days, you may want to use the system of putting meals for each day in a large plastic bag and labeling the bag with the date of use: "Wednesday, July 4." Within the large bag pack smaller bags labeled "Breakfast", "Lunch", and "Dinner." Leave the large bags in the trunk until the appropriate day.

Always know where your flashlight is. Try to bring one flashlight per person plus one for the "kitchen." It's a good idea to take a lot of matches; have a primary supply and put matches in several different places, just in case.

The most common mistake made by campers is to bring too much food. Although everyone tends to eat more when outdoors and exercising, be realistic.

Camping Equipment and Supplies

The right equipment can make a big difference in your campfire cooking experience. Although there is a wide range of equipment available from specialty suppliers, you should be able to get everything you need for cooking on a typical camping trip at the supermarket, the hardware store, and an outdoor equipment store – without spending a great deal of money. You'll probably find that everyday items such as aluminum foil and garbage bags are more important than a fancy new cooler.

Established campgrounds may have an installed fireplace, but you may need or want to bring a rack from home. An old refrigerator or oven rack will do nicely, you could bring the rack from your home grill, or you can buy small grills from an outdoor equipment store.

Start by getting a starter set of pots and pans for campfire cooking. You can find them in outdoor equipment stores in stainless steel or aluminum. Stainless steel is heavier and considerably more expensive than aluminum.

You'll need at least one 3 quart pot (two are better); and 8 to 9 quart pot the smaller pot can nest in (for steaming breads); a 10- to 12-inch non-stick skillet (the kind with handles that fold over are lightweight and pack easily); and a large coffee pot. Often you can get these pots and pans as sets that nest together in a single unit and include cups, metal plates, and lids that double as skillets.

(The skillets in these sets seldom have a non-stick coating, however, and you may regret not having it.) Look for pots with lids that have a snug fit, and buy pots with handles that can stand upright over the middle of the pot for lifting off a hot fire quickly.

Pots used on campfire will inevitably become blackened by the fire, but if you rub a coat of liquid soap on the outside of your pots and pans before you use them, they'll be easier to clean.

The long-handled cooking utensils you use for grilling at home are also good for campfire cooking. Regular cooking utensils are easier to use, however, so take both the long- and short-handled versions. A hinged, wire basket with a long handle works well for cooking fish, meat patties, and making toast. The nifty little Swiss Army knife is so handy you'll be using it constantly. Get the model with scissors, corkscrew, can opener and tweezers.

Dutch ovens made of cast iron are especially good for cooking in the coals because they're thick, heavy, and distribute heat evenly. They're also relatively inexpensive; get the kind with a flat, rimmed, metal (not glass) lid for holding coals, and follow the manufacturer's directions for seasoning it before the first use.

Bring plenty of drinking water containers on your camping trip. Look for plastic collapsible containers in outdoor equipment stores; they are inexpensive and pack into a small space. The kind with a tap and a carrying handle with a small hole that allows you to hang it from a tree are especially handy. Two 2 1/2 gallon containers are preferable to one 5 gallon size because carrying water will be easier and small containers tend to spring leaks less frequently. (The weight of the water probably explains why. Five gallons of water weighs 40 pounds.)

A length of plastic screen, which you can purchase from any hardware store, has many uses in camp. Put the screen over food to protect it from insects. The screen also makes a perfect "cupboard" for storing dishes after they're washed. Put the screen on the clothesline, folded in half lengthwise with the fold down, and fasten the two edges together and onto the clothesline with clothespins. This makes a long, open tube. Put dishes in either end; they dry quickly in their open air cupboard and are fairly well protected from insects as well.

Plastic garbage bags also have a number of uses. If it rains, they can be used for covering up gear and firewood. Cut holes for head and arms, and you have an emergency rain poncho. The 13 gallon size works nicely as a container for a big green salad. People have even been known to enjoy a hot bath in the heavy-duty, 30 gallon size. Just let the water heat up inside a black bag by setting it in the sun for a few hours.

Bring a roll of heavy-duty aluminum foil. You'll use it for cooking vegetables on the grill and in the coals, to make a tight seal for your pot when you steam breads, to heat up bread, as a makeshift plate, as a warming pan, and more. Don't forget the aluminum foil. It may well be the most indispensable item on your list.

Most campgrounds have large picnic tables, but you may very well camp in a place where there are no tables. There are several kinds of portable tables on the market. The compact, roll-up table with screw in legs is fairly sturdy and easy to transport, if you need to bring a table, don't forget to bring chairs!

Coolers, or ice chests, can keep food refrigerated for days. The cooler is kept cold with ice cubes, block ice, "blue ice", or ice that has been frozen in plastic bottles, milk cartons, or other containers. Blocks of ice and "blue ice" last far longer than do loose ice cubes.

Styrofoam camping coolers are inexpensive, but they are rather flimsy. They will do the job, but it seems that – inevitably – someone sits on the cooler and breaks it!

Metal coolers are heavily insulated, and will keep food colder and longer than foam or even the heavyweight plastic coolers. Metal coolers are the best and the most expensive.

Plastic coolers will keep food cold long enough for most camping trips, however. An excellent style features plastic bottles that screw into the inside of the lid. Freeze water in the bottles at home. Once affixed to the lid, they don't take up valuable space like block ice, and they don't make the melting mess that exposed ice does.

Keep all perishable food in your camp cooler. To slow bacteria growth you must maintain the cooler at a temperature of 40°F (4°C) or below. Open your camp cooler as few times as possible and do not leave it standing open. Try to keep your cooler in a shady area. Remove food from the cooler only when you are ready to serve it.

Camp Stoves

Although the recipes in this chapter were designed to be cooked over an open fire, you may find times when you need to use a camp stove on a camping trip. The chance of rain is, of course, a major consideration in planning to bring along a camp stove. The lack of rain,

which often results in a ban on open fires, is another reason to bring a stove. If you are camping in an area where gathering wood is prohibited, you may want to bring in a camp stove rather than carry in wood and charcoal briquettes. Or you may simply want to use the campfire as a supplement to the camp stove.

Be sure to check with the local authorities about the availability of wood for cooking when making your camping reservations.

First, decide how large you want your stove to be and what kind of fuel you prefer. For car camping you could get a large stove with several burners, or one or two small one burner backpacking stoves. Primary fuel choices are butane, propane, and white gas. Butane and propane stoves have fuel cartridges and usually are the easiest to light, but they can be finicky at high altitudes or on very cold mornings. Even though it takes a little practice to learn to light a white gas stove, many experienced camp cooks prefer them because white gas burns hotter and more efficiently than propane and butane. Moreover, finding the fuel cartridge that fits your particular butane or propane stove can be a problem, but white gas is readily available at camping supply stores and gasoline stations throughout North America.

Camping Equipment Checklist

You may not need every one of the items on this checklist of equipment every time you go camping. This equipment is enough to cook most meals, including those in the dinner and brunch recipes. Most of this equipment is found in home kitchens, and your regular equipment and utensils can, of course, double as your camping equipment. The problems of not having two sets are that you must pack up your outdoor kitchen every time you plan a trip and that it will suffer from use over an open fire.

It's really not necessary to bring an ax if you're gathering wood around the campsite. In fact, if you find you have to use an ax to get enough wood for your campfire, then wood is so scarce that it's ecologically unsound to gather wood for cooking. Do not assume there will be plenty of wood for a campfire. Bring wood and charcoal briquettes from home or use a camp stove.

If you use an ax to split wood, be aware that a long handled ax is safer than a short handled ax; If you miss your target with a long-handled ax, the blade is likely to bite harmlessly into the ground. The arc that a short-handled ax travels is a path that is liable to stop at your knee. So, be careful when chopping wood. Although a first aid kit is recommended, the hope is that you won't need it.

Emergency Equipment

Equip yourself properly for any emergency. In most areas it's against the law to have an open fire without a bucket and shovel nearby, and it is an excellent idea just all case. The United States Forest Service recommends that you keep a full bucket of water next to your campfire at all times. A garden shovel from home is fine, though shorter-handled camping shovels are easier to use.

Campfire Equipment

Water bottle with sprayer, for flare ups
Grilling rack
Bucket
Shovel
Long-handled axe
Wooden kitchen matches
Newspaper (to help start fire)
Fire starter, such as a candle (optional)
Oven mitts and hot pads
Matches

Cooking Equipment

2 three quart pots
1 eight quart pot
1 ten- or twelve-inch non stock skillet
1 one to twenty cup coffee pot
1 four quart Dutch oven (optional)
2 large metal spoons, with long handles
2 spatulas, with long handles
2 meat forks, one with a long handle
Wooden spoons
1 long-handled wire basket grill (optional)
Large tongs
Sharp knife
Swiss Army style knife, or be sure to include can opener, corkscrew, scissors and paring knife
Popcorn basket (optional)

Miscellaneous Equipment

Cooler
Water containers
Cutting board
Cheese grater
Strainer (for coffee grounds if you don't use filters)
Measuring cup
Measuring spoons
Plastic bottles
Plastic food tubes
Flashlight
Clothes pins
Clothesline
Plastic screen (about 3 by 6 feet)
Paper towels
Dish towels
Pre-soaped scrub sponge
Biodegradable soap
Plastic dish pan
Aluminum foil, heavy duty
Garbage bags, both 30 gallon and 10 gallon sizes
Sealable plastic bags, several sizes
Roll up table (optional)
Camp stove, fuel, funnel (optional)
First aid kit
Pump or water purifier
Insect repellent
Sun screen
Toilet paper
Safety pins and rubber bands
Sewing kit

Serving Equipment

Tablecloth, oilcloth is best
1 insulated cup per person
1 dinner sized plate per person
1 flatwear set per person
Paper napkins
Paper cups

First aid Kit

Assorted plastic bandages

Tape

Gauze

Elastic bandage

Tweezers

Scissors

Needle

Soap

Paper and pencil

Aspirin

Upset stomach remedy

Hydrocortisone cream

Antiseptic cream

Snakebite kit

Blister kit (especially if hiking)

Telephone number of nearest hospital

Telephone number of family doctor

First aid Kit

A good first aid kit is essential on a camping trip. You should also have a book on first aid. *Medicine for the Outdoors* by Paul S. Auerback, M.D. (Little, Brown and Company), is excellent, *Mountaineering Medicine, A Wilderness Medical Guide* by Fred T. Darvill Jr., M.D. (Seattle Mountaineers), is useful as well as small enough to fit into a first aid kit. Put together a kit of the basic supplies listed below and hope you won't need to open it. Don't forget to bring any prescription medicines members of your camping party may need.

Step by Step for Building a Fire and Making Coals

Gathering Wood

Firewood is often scarce, and wood gathering is banned in many areas. Check with local authorities about wood gathering and fire laws before you set up camp. You may not be allowed to have an open fire at all. You may need to bring charcoal briquettes or wood. If wood gathering is allowed, here are some tips on what to look for and what to avoid.

First, take wood only from the ground. Do not chop down trees or break off branches from standing trees. Avoid green wood; take dry wood that breaks easily. The kind of wood available is largely determined by where you are. If you have a choice, however, remember that hardwoods (oak, beech) make the best coals, and light woods such as pine and fir are best for starting a fire.

Wood that seems very lightweight is probably rotten. If it burns at all, it won't burn well. The thick bark of a large fallen fir can make good coals, but it depends on how long the tree has been down; it takes a hot, well-established fire to light the bark.

Gather wood in graduated sizes. You'll need tiny, dry twigs to start your fire, kindling to get it going, and larger sticks and logs to make good coals. Break the wood in sizes to accommodate your fireplace, and stack in bundles according to size at a convenient yet safe distance from the fire.

Don't gather more wood than you need. Keep your fire small. A small fire gives plenty of heat for cooking.

Building a Fireplace

If fireplaces are not provided in your campground, you can build one – or you can improve an existing fireplace by rearranging the stones. The size and type of fireplace you need will depend on what you're cooking, how you're cooking it, and the size of your group. Build a fire large enough for your needs, but no more. Your fireplace can be a simple trench, a fire ring, or an elaborate keyhole fireplace.

Trench Fireplace

To build a trench fireplace, you'll need to clear an area for your fire ring. Then, find four large, flat rocks. Dig a shallow trench in mineral soil, the layer below the organic soil. (Organic soil can burn and cause a fire to spread.) Make the trench about 2 feet long and narrower than the width of your grill rack. Leave the trench open at both ends to allow good air circulation, which will keep the fire burning efficiently. Place a rock on each side of the trench and balance the grill rack on top of the rocks, making sure the rack is stable. This fireplace is good for cooking simple meals for small groups, it can be built quickly, and it is easily dismantled. It's the best fireplace for "low impact camping."

Fire Ring

A fire ring is the classic campfire. Whenever possible use an established fire ring rather than building a new one. You do a service to the area by cleaning up a ruined fire ring and you'll make less of an impact on the environment. Make sure you place your fire ring on bare ground and that it is at least 100 feet back from your water source.

Start by clearing dead leaves and loose forest litter 10 feet back from where you want your fire. Then dig a shallow circular fireplace; you need to dig through the duff (the topsoil containing flammable organic material) and slightly down into the mineral soil. Next surround the fireplace with a shallow trench also dug down into the mineral soil. The moat will act as a firebreak, keeping sparks from the campfire from igniting the organic soil.

Now surround the fireplace circle with large rocks. Place the grill rack on top of the rocks, making sure the grill rack will be stable enough to hold several cooking pots. Use this fireplace for cooking and then remove the grill rack for after-dinner campfire watching.

Keyhole Fireplace

The keyhole fireplace is actually two fires, one for warming campers and baking food in the coals and a smaller fire to cook on that uses coals from the large fire. It's shaped like a keyhole and is an efficient arrangement for all campfire cooking methods. Clear an area as for a fire ring. Gather flat rocks and take care fitting them together. The round part of the keyhole should be large enough to accommodate the people in your group gathered around the fire, and the grill rack should fit well over the box shaped end. Flat rocks around the fire ring that are the size of your pots and skillet can be used for keeping food warm.

Making everything solid and level is one of the most important things to keep in mind when building a fireplace. Cooking on a campfire is a busy job, and the cook doesn't need the dangerous distraction of balancing pots of hot food on wobbly rocks.

When you leave your camp, it's fine to leave your fireplace up if it was already established. If you built your fireplace from scratch and the campsite was previously unused, however, dismantle your fireplace. Scatter the stones and turn the black, sooty side down to the ground and out of sight. All wood should be burned to ashes. Crush remaining coals and mix them together with mineral soil. Scatter this mixture around (making sure they are completely cold first). Make the area look as if no one has been there. We are guests in the wilderness, and the idea is to camp and leave no trace.

Lighting a Campfire

Lighting a campfire and keeping it going is a matter of giving it enough air by using tiny, dry sticks until the fire is established and then adding larger sticks at the right time. Most failed fires are a result of too much too soon. People start adding large sticks before the time is right, and the fire flickers and dies.

If you are building your fire in an established fireplace, make sure you clear away debris and burnt logs that may have been left by earlier campers. If you need to build a fireplace, see the description of different types on page 117. Before lighting any fire make sure you read the "Tips for Safe Campfire Cooking."

1. Start by crumpling tinder: newspapers, dry leaves, or pine needles. Then lay a pile of dry twigs (of matchstick size or smaller) or "furry sticks" on the tinder. (To make furry sticks, shave curls on the stick with a pocket knife and leave the shaving attached.)

2. Light the tinder and keep adding dry twigs or furry sticks to the burning pile. As the fire grows, you can lay on the small pieces of wood in a teepee or log cabin formation. The log cabin method develops the better bed of coals.

3. If the fire starts to go out, blow on it. When the fire is this small, it's safe to get very close to it and blow, and often that is what it takes. Be attentive and patient, and keep adding small twigs in a crisscross pattern around the flame. Gradually add larger twigs, then sticks as the fire builds up. Keep blowing on the fire when necessary until it's well established.

4. Once the fire is really going and you want to make a bed of coals, begin laying sticks and logs parallel and touching each other. They trap the heat and make the fire burn even hotter. Large sticks and logs burn down to coals. Dense wood makes better coals than softwood. Hardwoods, and sometimes thick fir or thick pine bark, can make good cooking coals. A wood fire will take from 30 to 60 minutes to burn down sufficiently for cooking.

5. Use caution when throwing loose paper, paper plates, or leaves on the fire or hot coals. A burst of wind could grab the burning paper and cause a fire. Never use lighter fluid to light wood or reignite coals. Read "Campfire Cooking Methods" below for information on how the coals should look before you begin cooking.

Campfire Cooking Methods

In learning to cook over coals from a wood fire, nothing is more important than experience. Even the most accomplished home chef who is used to a charcoal briquette fire can make mistakes at first. Here are some tips for successful campfire cooking.

First and foremost, never underestimate the heat of a wood fire. A direct flame should be used only for boiling. Realize, though, that coals will do the job just as well and without blackening the pots. Glowing coals are really too hot for baking. Use coals for grilling meat and, if you need to bake, wait until they burn down considerably. Charcoal briquettes do a fine job of grilling, but they burn too hot to make good coals for baking anything buried in them unless they're mixed with wood coals, embers, and ashes.

Second, you must remember to feed the fire. It's easy to get involved in your cooking and forget that you're not at home on the range. Try to cook with the lid on pots – food will heat faster and you will save fuel.

Campfire Baking in the Coals

You need to use a Dutch oven or an aluminum foil-capped skillet to bake in the campfire coals. You can bake just about anything; beans, brownies, breads, and all sorts of desserts. The secret is to make sure the coals are not too hot. Good baking coals may seem a bit past their prime. They're mixed with ashes, and you should be able to hold your hand over them for several seconds. The fire ring is a good place to bake when the fire has been burning for a long time because there is a deep pile of coals and ashes. Bury the Dutch oven, shovel coals on the lid, and check the food often if you're in doubt. If you're using a skillet, cap it with a double or triple layer of heavy-duty aluminum foil and put coals over it. After a little practice judging the temperature of coals, you'll be turning out perfectly fine baked goods.

Campfire Steaming

Breads and cakes will be moister when steamed than when baked in the coals. They will take longer to cook, but seldom burn (unless you let the water boil away). Steaming is also a cooking method you can use on the camp stove when open fires are prohibited. Since things take quite awhile to cook when using the steam method, it's usually not a good idea to double a recipe.

You'll need two pots, one that nests inside the other with about $1/2$ inch to spare around the edge. Oil the inside of the smaller pot, pour in the batter, and seal tightly. Place inside the larger pot. Add water to the larger pot until the surface is a couple of inches below the lip of the smaller pot. If pots are thin, use a metal plate or crumpled aluminum foil to separate them at the bottom and use both aluminum foil and the lid for a good seal. Keep the water boiling steadily for the recommended baking time. Try not to peek until the time is up, and even then you may have to cook it longer.

Buried Cooking

You can cook potatoes, yams, whole onions, sweet potatoes, and other vegetables by burying them in the coals in their jackets or wrapping them in heavy-duty aluminum foil. There is less of a chance of burning buried food than baked, but you still have to be cautious about not using glowing, red coals. If you're not careful, you'll burn the vegetables. Be cautious when working near hot coals. Make sure to wear fireproof mitts and use a long-handled spoon or camping shovel to bury and uncover food.

High Altitude Cooking

If you make your camp at 8,000 feet or higher, you'll notice that everything takes longer to cook. This is because water boils at a lower temperature when atmospheric pressure is lower. Water doesn't have to reach the sea level boiling point of 212°F (100°C) before it begins to bubble; water boils at 196°F (91°C) at 8,000 feet, and at 194°F (90°C) at 10,000 feet.

How do these facts affect specific foods? Pasta, for example, requires very hot, boiling water to cook well. As a result, it's usually not a good idea to plan a dried pasta meal at high elevation (fresh pasta, however, just needs to cook a bit longer). Some cooks have moderate success with commercial dried pasta at 9,000 feet by using furiously boiling water, a high water to pasta ratio, and cooking it longer – but it really does turn to wallpaper paste when cooked at altitudes higher than 9,000 feet.

You'll also have trouble cooking rice, bulgur wheat, and any grains by standard methods at high altitude. Outdoor equipment stores sell little camping pressure cookers; they really do work, and they save fuel too.

Breads and cakes can even behave differently at 4,000 feet. You'll need to use slightly less leavening and sugar and slightly more liquid and flour. At 8,000 feet, increase the baking temperature by 25°F (10°C), and they will still take longer to cook. Butter pots well – cakes and breads stick more at high altitudes.

At very high elevations (9,000 to 10,000 feet), you may experience a loss of appetite, and food you usually love to eat just doesn't taste as good. Eat anyway, and drink a lot of water. Be sure to encourage children to drink water and juices when camping at high elevations. Bring packages of dried drink mixes to add to water that may not taste good to you; they also help cover the taste of water treatment products. Make sure you bring along soups and herb teas, which become especially appealing at high altitudes.

Basics About Water

Water is usually plentiful, but if you have a "dry camp," you'll need to bring water for doing dishes, putting out the campfire, cooking, drinking, and washing. The amount of drinking water you'll need depends on how active you are and on the weather. In hot weather, hikers should consume a gallon of water per day. You can easily become dehydrated yet not feel thirsty, so drink lots of water when you're living outdoors – especially if you're at high elevations where the air is always very dry.

If you need to bring in your water, a good rule of thumb is to bring 2 gallons of water per person per day.

Remember that the melted ice in the camp cooler is perfectly good water for many camp-site clean-up chores. Be sure to check on water availability when making camping reservations and plan accordingly.

Giardia Is Not A Pasta Dish

Always make sure that there is water available at your campsite and that the water is safe to drink. If you are not sure, bring plenty of water with you for cooking and drinking. Most established campgrounds have tap water, which is perfectly safe for drinking. However, if you're getting your drinking and cooking water from a stream, lake, or spring, purify the water to protect yourself from the risk of ingesting organisms that will make you sick. *Giardia lamblia*, a parasite that inhabits the lower intestine, is of particular concern because it has become quite prevalent in the United States in the last 10 years. The symptoms, which may take from 3 days to a month to manifest, are diarrhea, stomach cramps, flatulence, and sometimes vomiting. If you experience these symptoms after drinking from an unusual water source, seek a doctor's care.

Water Purification

There are three ways to effectively purify water so that it is safe to drink:

1. Boil water for 5 minutes.

2. You can buy a filter pump from an outdoor equipment store. You need at least a 0.4 micron filter to keep the *giardia* cysts from passing through.

3. Treat water with iodine. Add 10 drops (no more) of a 2 percent tincture of iodine to a quart of water and wait

30 minutes before dinking it. Don't forget to pour some of the treated water around the threads and on the lid of your water bottle so any organisms on them don't contaminate the purified water. If you add lemonade or something else to mask the taste of the iodine, don't add it until the 30 minutes have elapsed; vitamin C can counteract the action of the iodine.

There are commercial pills containing iodides that also work against *giardia* but they're much more expensive than a 2 percent tincture of iodine. In addition, if the pills are not used within a few weeks of opening the bottle, they begin to oxidize and become ineffective. Be warned: bleach, halazone, pills and other products that do not contain iodide are often sold as water purifiers. Although they clean the water of some pollutants, they do not protect you against *giardia*.

Basics of Barbecue Sauces

Sauces reflect both regional variety and individual taste. Families and barbecue houses jealously guard their "secret" recipe. Experiment with the recipes that follow and alter them to suit your own taste. Most of these recipes aren't spicy hot – this lets you taste the basic sauce for the balance of sweet and sour. Once satisfied with the base, you can spice it up with cayenne pepper, chiles, jalapenos, hot pepper sauce, or the like. If you are serving a lot of people, make a mild or moderately spicy sauce, then let the daring ones in the crowd spice up their plate by sprinkling on crushed cayenne pepper or hot pepper sauce. Barbecue sauces will keep for up to a week refrigerated and freeze well for several months.

Georgia Sauce

Plain and easy to prepare, this sauce is a good choice for a mixed crowd with various tastes. For those who like hot food, put crushed red pepper and a bottle of hot sauce on the table. This sauce works equally well with beef, pork, chicken, and fish.

1½ cups tomato puree
1 cup cider vinegar
½ cup oil
⅓ cup Worcestershire Sauce
½ cup firmly-packed dark brown sugar
¼ cup molasses
3 tbsps mustard
2 tsps minced garlic
1 lemon, juiced

In a large non aluminum saucepan, combine all ingredients. Slowly simmer for 15 minutes. Stir often to prevent sauce from burning. Allow sauce to rest for at least 1 hour after cooking to allow flavors to meld. Store in covered container in refrigerator until used.
Makes 3 cups

North Carolina Sauce

In eastern Northern Carolina, barbecue is taken very seriously. The simplicity of slowly roasted meat is accented only with the addition of crushed red peppers and cider vinegar–you won't fine tomato sauce. At the table there is always a bottle of plain cider vinegar next to the bottle of barbecue sauce.

1 cup cider vinegar
2 tbsps crushed red pepper
1 tsp liquid hot pepper sauce

Place all ingredients in a small plastic or glass container. Cover and shake well to combine. Store in refrigerator until used.
Makes 1 cup

Texas Sauce

This is a very rich and complexly flavored sauce, full of vegetables and perfumed with chile powder and a hint of cumin. Oddly enough, there is no mustard in this sauce, so the flavor of tomato comes out more distinctly than in many barbecue sauces. This sauce is an excellent choice for beef, pork, and chicken. Don't use it on fish – it will easily overpower the delicate flavor.

½ cup butter
1 cup onion, finely chopped
1 cup celery, finely chopped
2 tsps minced garlic
1 cup tomato puree
½ cup cider vinegar
½ cup firmly-packed dark brown sugar
1 cup beef stock
¼ cup Worcestershire sauce
2 bay leaves
2 tsps freshly ground black pepper
2 tsps cayenne pepper
1 tsp ground cumin
2 tsps chili powder
salt, to taste

In a large non-aluminum saucepan, melt butter and saute onion, celery and garlic until soft (about 10 minutes). Add remaining ingredients and slowly simmer for about 30 minutes. Stir frequently so that sauce doesn't burn. Allow sauce to rest for at least 1 hour so that flavors meld. Store covered in refrigerator. This sauce is even better the following day.
Makes 4 cups

Kansas City Sauce

In Kansas City, they love smoke and they love a thick and sweet sauce. The liquid smoke flavorin, recreated the smoky flavor of meat slowly smoked in the famous Kansas City barbecue pits. Ketchup, molasses, and yellow mustard combine to lay the foundation for this thick all American sauce. If you like spicy barbecue, try adding 1 to 2 tablespoons ground cayenne pepper. This sauce works well with beef, pork, or chicken; it would overpower fish.

½ cup oil
1 onion, finely chopped
½ green bell pepper, finely chopped
2 tsps minced garlic
1 bottle (16oz) ketchup
½ cup molasses
2 tsps hot pepper sauce
¼ cup yellow mustard
2 tbsps cider vinegar
½ cup firmly-packed dark brown sugar
4 tbsps Worcestershire sauce
1 tsp liquid smoke flavor
¼ cup fresh lemon juice

Place oil in a large non-aluminum saucepan, then saute onion, green pepper, and garlic until soft (about 10 minutes). Add remaining ingredients and continue to simmer slowly for 20 to 30 minutes. Stir frequently to prevent sauce from burning. Let rest for at least 1 hour after cooking to allow the flavors to meld.
Makes 4 cups

Louisiana Sauce

In Louisiana, barbecue sauce begins in the same manner as other Creole sauces by employing the classic combination of onions, celery, green bell peppers, tomato and garlic. The Creole recipe adds thyme and oregano at this point; create a barbecue sauce by adding molasses, brown sugar, and vinegar. This recipe produces a spicy, thick, complexly flavored sauce suitable for almost any cut of beef, pork, chicken, or fish. Louisiana natives may add more cayenne than this recipe calls for to make a memorably fiery sauce.

1 cup oil
2 cups finely chopped onion
1 large green bell pepper, finely chopped
1 cup celery, finely chopped
2 tbsps minced garlic
2 cups tomato puree
1 tbsp Creole or Dijon mustard
¼ cup white vinegar
4 tsps cayenne pepper
1 tsp hot pepper sauce
1 bay leaf
2 tsps freshly ground black pepper
½ cup firmly packed dark brown sugar
¼ cup dark molasses

Place oil in a large non-aluminum saucepan, then saute onion, bell pepper, celery, and garlic until soft (about 10 minutes). Add remainder of ingredients and simmer slowly for 10 to 15 minutes, stirring frequently to avoid burning. Adjust seasoning to taste by altering amounts of sugar, spices, and vinegar. Cook an additional 5 to 10 minutes after changing seasoning. Let rest for at least 1 hour after cooking to allow flavors to meld. Store covered in refrigerator. Sauce is even better the next day.
Makes 6 cups

Bourbon Sauce

This sauce works equally well as a basting sauce and as a marinade. The alcohol evaporates as the sauce cooks, leaving a mysterious and intense bittersweet flavor. To use as a marinade, coat meat and leave covered in the refrigerator for 8 to 12 hours. Continue to baste with sauce as meat cooks, but don't serve this on the side – it is really only suitable if cooked into the meat. Sauce works best with pork and beef.

2 tbsps lard
1 onion, finely chopped
1 tbsp minced garlic
2 cups tomato puree
½ cup Worcestershire sauce
2 tbsps cider vinegar
½ cup yellow mustard
½ cup firmly-packed brown sugar
¼ cup bourbon
2 tbsps each hot red chile powder and mild red chile powder
2 drops liquid smoke flavor

Place lard in a large non aluminum saucepan and saute onion and garlic until soft (about 10 minutes). Add remaining ingredients and continue to cook for an additional 30 minutes. If you can't find the two strengths of chile powder, substitute 3 tablespoons ground cayenne pepper total. Stir frequently to prevent sauce from burning. Allow to rest for at least 1 hour before using.
Makes 3 cups

King Sauce

This recipe was contributed by Oakland, California, artist John King. The nature of the sauce is predominantly Asian, but there are a few interesting western touches. Use this sauce as a marinade for your barbecue and as a basting sauce. Rub the sauce into the meat and refrigerate covered for 8 to 12 hours. This sauce goes particularly well with pork and beef but can also be used with chicken and fish.

2 cups hoisin sauce
1 cup soy sauce
2 tbsps each white vinegar and dry sherry
4 tbsps sesame oil
4 tbsps Dijon mustard
1 lemon, juiced
pepper, to taste

1 tsp ground cumin
2 tsps fennel seed, crushed
2 tsps mirin
⅓ cup orange juice

In a large bowl combine all ingredients and mix well. Adjust sauce to taste by altering individual amounts of each ingredient. The flavors tend to dilute considerably during cooking, so keep them strong.
Makes 8 cups

Florida Sauce

This unusual barbecue sauce includes horseradish and lime juice. It is tangy and sweet, with a delicate taste and a short shelf life. Try to make this the same day as your barbecue because the flavors tend to fade quickly. This sauce is excellent on fish and chicken, and interesting on pork. It is too delicate to match with beef ribs.

1 cup unsalted butter
½ cup firmly-packed dark brown sugar
1 cup tomato puree
½ cup cider vinegar
¾ cup prepared horseradish
½ cup fresh lime juice
1 tbsp Worcestershire sauce
2 tsps hot pepper sauce

In a large non-aluminum saucepan, melt butter and add remaining ingredients. Simmer slowly for 20 to 25 minutes, stirring frequently to prevent sauce from burning. Sauce can be used immediately.
Makes 4 cups

Marinating

Marinating foods has two purposes. First, to impart delightful flavors and second, but equally important, to tenderize the meats. The following points will guide you.

Honey and Lemon Marinade

$^1/_2$ cup olive oil
2 tbsps lemon juice
1 tbsp honey
1 tbsp garlic freshly crushed
2 bay leaves, crushed
Method: Mix all ingredients together.

Teriyaki Marinade

$^1/_2$ cup soy sauce
2 tbsps brown sugar
$^1/_2$ tsp ground ginger
2 tbsps wine vinegar
1 clove garlic, crushed
2 tbsps tomato sauce
Method: Mix all ingredients together.

Herbed Wine Marinade

$^1/_2$ cup white wine
1 tbsp honey
2 tbsps salad oil
3 sprigs fresh thyme or majoram
1 clove garlic, finely chopped
Method: Mix all ingredients well together.

Honey and Chili Marinade

$^1/_4$ cup red wine
$^1/_2$ cup honey
$^1/_4$ tsp ground chili
1 tsp mustard powder
Method: Mix well together.

Tandoori Paste

2 cloves garlic, peeled
1in peeled fresh ginger chopped
1 tsp salt
2 tsps cilantro seeds
2 tbsps lemon juice
2 tbsps vinegar
1 tsp cumin seeds
$^1/_2$ tsp chili powder
1 tsp turmeric
$^1/_2$ cup plain yogurt
Method: Blend all ingredients except the yogurt in an electric blender to a smooth paste. Stir into the yoghurt.

Red Wine and Garlic Marinade

$^1/_2$ cup red wine
2 tbsps brown sugar
2 cloves garlic, crushed
salt, pepper
Method: Mix all ingredients together.

Satay Marinade

$^1/_2$ cup peanut butter
$^1/_2$ tsp chili powder
$^1/_2$ tsp ground ginger
2 tbsps lemon juice
1 tbsp brown sugar
$^1/_2$ cup coconut milk
Method: Place all ingredients in a pan, heat and stir to combine.

Ginger-Rum Marinade

$^1/_2$ cup unsweeted pineapple
$^3/_8$ cup light rum
$^1/_4$ cup soy sauce
1 tbsp ginger, chopped
2 tsps garlic, crushed
1 tbsp brown sugar
$^1/_4$ tsp chili powder
Method: Mix all ingredients together.

Lime-Garlic Marinade

$^1/_2$ cup chicken stock
2 tbsps lime juice
2 tbsps olive oil
1 tbsp brown sugar
3 tsps crushed garlic
$^1/_4$ tsp chili powder
$^1/_4$ tsp mint flakes
or $^1/_2$ tsp chopped fresh mint
Method: Mix all ingredients together.

Soy and Honey Marinade

$^1/_4$ cup soy sauce
2 tbsps honey
1 tbsp sherry
2 cloves garlic, crushed
1 tsp fresh ginger, grated
Method: Mix all ingredients together.

Weights & Measures

Cooking is not an exact science: one does not require finely-calibrated scales, pipettes and scientific equipment to cook, yet the conversion to metric measures in some countries and its interpretations must have intimidated many a good cook.

Weights are given in the recipes only for ingredients such as meats, fish, poultry and some vegetables. Though a few ounces /grams one way or another will not affect the success of your dish

Though recipes have been tested using the Australian Standard 250 mL cup, 20 mL tablespoon and 5 mL teaspoon, they will work just as well with the US and Canadian 8 fl oz cup, or the UK 300 mL cup. We have used graduated cup measures in preference to tablespoon measures so that proportions are always the same. Where tablespoon measures have been given, these are not crucial measures, so using the smaller tablespoon of the US or UK will not affect the recipe's success. At least we all agree on the teaspoon size.

For breads, cakes and pastries, the only area which might cause concern is where eggs are used, as proportions will then vary. If working with a 250 mL or 300 mL cup, use large eggs 2 oz (60g), adding a little more liquid to the recipe for 300mL cup measures if it seems necessary. Use the medium-sized eggs 1^{1}/4oz (55g) with 8 fl oz cup measure. A graduated set of measuring cups and spoons is recommended, the cups in particular for measuring dry ingredients. Remember to level such ingredients to ensure their accuracy.

English measures

All measurements are similar to Australian with two exceptions: the English cup measures 10 fl oz (300 mL), whereas the Australian cup measure 8 fl oz (250 mL).

The English tablespoon (the Australian dessertspoon) measures ^{1}/2fl oz (14.8mL) against the Australian tablespoon of ^{3}/4fl oz (20mL).

American measures

The American reputed pint is 16 fl oz, a quart is equal to 32 fl oz and the American gallon, 128 fl oz. The Imperial measurement is 20 fl oz to the pint, 40 fl oz a quart and 160 fl oz one gallon. The American tablespoon is equal to ^{1}/2 fl oz (14.8 mL), the teaspoon is ^{1}/6 fl oz/5 mL. The cup measure is 250 mL (8 fl oz) (this really is 8^{3}/4 fl oz, however in most cases as a cooks measurement the 8 fl oz (250 mL) applies) the same as Australia.

Dry measures

All the measures are level, so when you have filled a cup or spoon, level it off with the edge of a knife. The scale that follows is the "cook's equivalent;" it is not an exact conversion of metric to imperial measurement. To calculate the exact metric equivalent yourself, use 2.2046 lb = 1 kg or 1 lb = 0.45359 kg.

Weights & measures

Dry measures

Metric	Imperial
g = grams	oz = ounces
kg = kilograms	lb = pound
15 g	$^1/_2$oz
20 g	$^2/_3$oz
30 g	1 oz
55 g	2 oz
85 g	3 oz
115 g	4 oz/$^1/_4$ lb
145 g	5 oz
170 g	6 oz
200 g	7 oz
225 g	8 oz/$^1/_2$ lb
255 g	9 oz
285 g	10 oz
315 g	11 oz
340 g	12 oz/ $^3/_4$ lb
370 g	13 oz
400 g	14 oz
425 g	15 oz
455 g	16o z/1 lb
1,000 g/1 kg	35.2 oz/2.2 lbs

Cake dish sizes

metric	imperial
15cm	6in
18cm	7in
20cm	8in
23cm	9in

Loaf dish sizes

metric	imperial
23 x 12cm	9 x 5in
25 x 8cm	10 x 3in
28 x 18cm	11 x 7in

Oven temperatures

The Celsius temperatures given here are not exact; they have been rounded off and are given as a guide only. Follow the manufacturer's temperature guide, relating it to oven description given in the recipe. Remember gas ovens are hottest at the top, electric ovens at the bottom and convection-fan forced ovens are usually even throughout. We included Regulo numbers for gas cookers which may assist. To convert °C to °F multiply °C by 9 and divide by 5 then add 32.

Oven temperatures

	C°	F°	REGULO
Very slow	125	250	1
Slow	150	300	2
Moderately slow	160	325	3
Moderate	180	350	4
Moderately hot	190 - 200	370 - 400	5 - 6
Hot	210 - 220	410 - 440	6 - 7
Very hot	230	450	8
Super hot	250 - 290	475 - 500	9 - 10

Liquid measures

metric	imperial	cup and spoon
mL	fl oz	
millilitres	fluid ounce	
5 mL	$^1/_6$ fl oz	1 teaspoon
20 mL	$^2/_3$ fl oz	1 tablespoon
30 mL	1 fl oz	1 tablespoon plus 2 teaspoons
55 mL	2 fl oz	$^1/_4$ cup
70 mL	2 $^1/_2$fl oz	$^1/_3$ cup
85 mL	3 fl oz	$^3/_8$ cup
115 mL	4 fl oz	$^1/_2$ cup
145 mL	5 fl oz	$^1/_4$ pint, 1 gill
225 mL	8 fl oz	1 cup

Liquid measures

metric	imperial	cup and spoon
mL	fl oz	
millilitres	fluid ounce	
300 mL	10 fl oz	$^1/_2$ pint
360 mL	12 fl oz	$1^1/_2$ cups
420 mL	14 fl oz	$1^3/_4$ cups
500 mL	16 fl oz	2 cups
600 mL	20 fl oz /1 pint	$2^1/_2$ cups
1 litre	35 fl oz/ $1^3/_4$ pints	4 cups

Cup measurements

One cup is equal to the following weights:

	Metric	Imperial
Almonds, flaked	90 g	3 oz
Almonds, slivered, ground	125 g	4 oz
Almonds, kernel	155 g	5 oz
Apples, dried, chopped	125 g	4 oz
Apricots, dried, chopped	190 g	6 oz
Breadcrumbs, packet	125 g	4 oz
Breadcrumbs, soft	60 g	2 oz
Cheese, grated	125 g	4 oz
Choc bits	155 g	5 oz
Coconut, desiccated	90 g	3 oz
Cornflakes	30 g	1 oz
Currants	155 g	5 oz
Flour	125 g	4 oz
Fruit, dried (mixed, sultanas etc)	185 g	6 oz
Ginger, crystallised, glace	250 g	8 oz
Honey, treacle, golden syrup	315 g	10 oz
Mixed peel	220 g	7 oz
Nuts, chopped	125 g	4 oz
Prunes, chopped	220 g	7 oz
Rice, cooked	155 g	5 oz
Rice, uncooked	220 g	7 oz
Rolled oats	90 g	3 oz
Sesame seeds	125 g	4 oz
Shortening (butter, margarine)	250 g	8 oz
Sugar, brown	155 g	5 oz
Sugar, granulated or caster	250 g	8 oz
Sugar, sifted icing	155 g	5 oz
Wheatgerm	60 g	2 oz

Length

Some of us still have trouble converting imperial length to metric. In this scale, measures have been rounded off to the easiest-to-use and most acceptable figures. To obtain the exact metric equivalent in converting inches to centimetres, multiply inches by 2.54 whereby 1 inch equals 25.4 millimetres and 1 millimetre equals 0.03937 inches.

Metric	Imperial
mm=millimetres	in = inches
cm=centimetres	ft = feet
5mm/0.5cm	$^1/_4$in
10mm/1.0cm	$^1/_2$in
20mm/2.0cm	$^3/_4$in
2.5cm	1in
5cm	2in
8cm	3in
10cm	4in
12cm	5in
15cm	6in
18cm	7in
20cm	8in
23cm	9in
25cm	10in
28cm	11in
30cm	1ft/12in

Index

ALSO BY K. KRIS LOOMIS

NONFICTION

How to Sneak More Yoga Into Your Life: A Doable Yoga Plan for Busy
People

How to Sneak More Meditation Into Your Life: A Doable Meditation Plan
for Busy People

Thirty Days In Quito: Two Gringos and a Three-Legged Cat Move to
Ecuador

FICTION

The Park Stories (Modern Shorts for Busy People Book 1)

The Cafe Stories (Modern Shorts for Busy People Book 2)

The Funeral Home Stories (Modern Shorts for Busy People Book 3)

The Bus Stories (Modern Shorts for Busy People Book 4)

The Bedroom Stories (Modern Shorts for Busy People Book 5)

The Monster In the Closet and Other Stories (Modern Shorts for Busy
People Books 1 - 5)

For my students, from whom I've learned a lot.

Author's Note

I published my first two books about yoga and meditation in the spring of 2016. And while I did offer personal anecdotes as examples, these books are mostly instructional in nature, where I offer people specific ways they can incorporate more yoga and mindfulness into their life, no matter how busy they are.

After I designed my author website, though, I wrote several personal articles and essays about yoga and meditation and published them on my blog. Those posts go deeper into how the study of yoga has altered the course of my thinking, and ultimately, the direction of my life. Many of the essays in *After Namaste* have been adapted from those writings.

I would like to thank my first reader, Hugh Loomis, for his honesty, love, and never-ending encouragement.

After Namaste: Introduction

"Namaste," says the teacher at the end of class.
"Namaste," you reply.

You just had a great yoga class and you feel fantastic. Pumped! Perhaps even a bit inspired.

So now what? What happens after namaste?

What happens after namaste depends on where you are on your yoga journey. What happens after namaste depends on where you are on your personal journey. What happens after namaste depends on how you begin to blend those two journeys together.

When I began studying yoga, I was pretty much content to go to class and then go home. I considered my time on the mat to be separate from the rest of my life.

But yoga is a sneaky practice. Before long, I

realized I was applying things I had learned on the mat to other aspects of my life. From simply being more aware of my surroundings to taking personal responsibility for my words and actions, I couldn't deny that my yoga journey was slowly merging with my personal one.

And while yoga has given me tools to cope with stressful situations, to honestly assess challenges, to step out of the "drama zone" and dig a little deeper, I will admit that I am not always "yoga-like" in my response to life's "un-pretty" moments. To say my journey has not always been neat and predictable would be an understatement.

But yoga has taught me it's never too late to reassess a situation and learn from it, even if I have to learn the lesson over (and over) again. Yoga has taught me it's never too late to better myself, no matter what is right or wrong in the world around me. Yoga has taught me that change begins with *me*, by accepting what I *can* control (*my* actions and attitudes) and not getting derailed by what I *can't* control (*other* people's actions and attitudes).

This collection of musings is a reflection of how my study of yoga has affected me off the mat as a teacher, as a student, and as a regular person dealing with the ups and downs of life. You will find

my thoughts about yoga, but I've also included some thoughts about other things as well, like quotes, housework, pets, and dealing with unexpected (and often unwanted) changes in life because my thoughts about *many* things have been shaped by my time on the mat.

I hope this book will encourage you to think about yoga in a new way, to see that yoga is not just something you do on the mat, to incorporate the lessons you learn during practice into the rest of your life.

The lessons I've learned so far on my yoga journey inspire me to return to the mat day after day because I know I've only scratched the surface. You see, I am a yogini in progress, a person still learning, still intrigued, and ever thankful for what happens after namaste.

A Swimmer's Meditation

Many years ago, after finding myself at a mid-life crossroad after an unpleasant divorce, I bought a townhouse. It was a small, two-bedroom townhouse, which was great because I didn't want to have to take care of a lot of stuff. The HOA dues covered all of the outside yard maintenance, and that was fine with me. I wanted to think, not mow grass. The dues also covered the use of the community pool.

Now, I am a reader, not a swimmer, but I found myself drawn to the pool often. I would sit with a book in hand, just far enough away from the swimmers and splashers, and enjoy the opportunity to observe human interactions from a safe distance behind my sunglasses. Young kids in their colorful water wings, awkward teenagers, middle-aged

sunbathers, gym rats, school swimmers, I saw a lot of different types of people there.

I loved going to the pool in the mornings before the bright Carolina sun became too hot, forcing me to jump in to cool off. Like I said, I'm not a swimmer.

One morning while I was reading the latest Ken Follett book, a man I had never seen before entered through the main gate at the other end of the pool. He was lean, sinewy, and practically bald. Serious-looking goggles hung loosely around his neck, and his black, tight suit was much smaller than the knee-length "dad trunks" I was accustomed to seeing in the neighborhood.

I observed him as he moved to the edge of the pool, did a few shoulder rolls, moved his head from side to side a couple of times, then dove headfirst into the pool, going the entire length without coming up for air. When he got to the other end, he adjusted his goggles, then proceeded to teach me a thing or two about yoga.

What struck me at first was the beauty of his stroke. He swam freestyle the entire time, but it was almost as if he were moving in slow motion. His movements were controlled and precise. Beautiful, really. His flip turns at the wall were so perfectly

timed that he never skipped a beat once he re-emerged. He continued at exactly the same pace he had set at the beginning.

As I continued watching this stranger, I noticed that it looked like he never came up for air. His head turn was so slight and fluid that I had to look hard to see it. He didn't raise his head, just barely turned it into what I would later find out was called "the pocket." There were hardly any ripples as he glided gracefully through the water for thirty minutes straight, not once stopping or changing his pace.

I was transfixed. Watching him became a meditation, for everything else around the pool disappeared that morning.

After exactly half an hour the man got out of the pool, picked up his towel, slipped on his flip-flops, and left. I never saw him again.

The next morning I rolled out my yoga mat in the kitchen (which doubled as my yoga room). I stood at the top of my mat with my hands in Anjali mudra, the prayer position, and closed my eyes. I remembered the calm serenity of the swimmer. The deliberate and delicate movements. The precision of his breath. How his physical movements seemed to be perfectly married to his inhalations and

exhalations. I opened my eyes and began my practice.

I did nothing but sun salutations that morning, trying to emulate the smooth transitions the swimmer had demonstrated the day before. I imagined that the air around me had mass, providing me with a little resistance, like that of the water in a pool. I worked hard to match my movements to my breath, and even harder to keep my breath perfectly even. I slowed everything down, *way* down. And because I was moving and breathing so slowly, I had a chance to really observe my form. Come to find out, I had gotten a little sloppy with a few things, especially my foot placement and alignment. I began to tweak a little here and there, and after about thirty sun salutations felt like I was finally in a groove.

Funny thing was, the longer I practiced, the stronger I felt. I did not get winded or lose my breath. I experienced a deep calm that I never imagined possible after working so long at repeating the same movements over and over. I realized my practice that morning had become a lovely, slow-motion meditation reminiscent of the swimmer.

One of the things I took from that experience is that teachers can be found anywhere if we are

willing to recognize them when they present themselves. That swimmer altered more than my personal practice; he also changed the way I approach teaching. I'm sure he had no idea that his discipline affected me so deeply that warm summer morning, but that in itself was a bigger lesson.

Never underestimate the power of example, for you never know who may be watching.

A Simple Intention

Intentions. The road to hell is paved with 'em. They can be good. They can be bad. We often hide behind them. Sometimes we wear them like badges. They can distract us or bring about laser focus. They can be frivolous or deadly serious. You can even go to prison because of them.

As a student and teacher of yoga, I have often struggled with the meaning of the word "intention." Are intentions enough? How do I decide on one in class? In relationships? In life? Can't I just do stuff and hope for the best?

I have attended many yoga classes through the years that begin with the call to "set your intention for class." What the heck does that even mean exactly? I always figured my intention needed to be something big, like world peace, or dedicating my

practice to the victims of (insert disaster of the day) because teachers are so solemn when they ask you to do it.

Now, I'm not saying that sympathy and well wishes are not necessary or appreciated. But I spent some time living in a South American country during a period when some of the most devastating earthquakes shook that part of the earth, and I can tell you first hand that the people of Ecuador would much rather have clean water and funds to rebuild their infrastructure than my really good down dog and useless intentions.

So how can you set reasonable and attainable intentions?

I believe the answer lies in simplicity. The smaller and more specific the intention, the more likely you are to see it through. We all have dreams and goals, but those aims are made up of many, much smaller units of measurement.

When I started studying yoga, my intention was to become better at yoga. But after about a year I really wasn't that much better than when I began even though I had been going to class on a regular basis. I had the intention, but nothing had changed to put me closer to my goal. My intention was too imprecise, too grand.

In my second year of studying yoga, I decided to pick just one specific intention for each class and practice. And no, not once did it involve world peace. My intentions were much smaller in scale. Some examples:

- I will not clench my teeth during this class.
- I will keep my breath steady for twenty minutes.
- I will bring my attention back to my practice each time it wanders.
- I will not stare at the new, really flexible student in the front row. (And I will definitely not be jealous!)
- I will keep the mound at the base of my index finger securely on the mat while in down dog.
- I will at least *try* to engage my bandhas throughout the Ashtanga standing sequence during this practice.
- I will calmly step out of my comfort zone and produce at least one good, clear OM.

Now, these are not earth-shattering intentions, but over time these smaller intentions did, in fact, lead me to my larger goal of becoming better at

yoga. An extra benefit was this process gave me a template to use while off the mat in my "real" life, as well.

I believe the goal of a better world is attainable one simple intention at a time. Instead of just thinking about a problem and feeling overwhelmed, I now look for small, specific ways to inch toward my goal. If we were all content with following through on just a few small intentions, those smaller, focused intentions would add up and lead to much larger and positive changes on, and off, the mat.

Things I Learned from a Set of Footprints in the Sand

My husband and I recently had the opportunity to spend a long weekend at a friend's beach house on the Isle of Palm in South Carolina. I love Carolina beaches. To me, there is nothing quite as lovely as kicking off your shoes under a bright Carolina blue sky and walking slowly beside the foamy water while holding the hand of someone you love.

I love getting up early to do a little yoga on the beach before the rest of the world is awake. I find yoga in the sand to be quite challenging, but I love it. And I savor the opportunity to walk on the beach because I can always incorporate an element of meditation on the stroll.

On one of our daily walks on the beach that weekend, I decided to focus on the many different footprints we came across. I have always enjoyed looking at footprints in the sand. I like to guess what the person who passed before me looked like, dressed like, carried with them to the shore. What did they think about out here on the beach? Did they read or watch people? Were they happy? Did they walk the beach for much-needed alone time or walk with a friend or lover? Why did this person walk barefooted and this one wear shoes?

Because it was off-season, most of the footprints I saw while walking the beach that day were made by residents. Many of those full-timers had their dogs with them, and because there were few people out in the chilly fall air, most of the dogs were allowed to run off leash.

After we had been walking awhile, I noticed two interesting sets of footprints. The first set was made by a two-legged creature walking in a straight line, but the second set was snaky and unpredictable and often intersected the straight line with its four paws. I was sure the human and the canine would end up at the same place eventually, but they sure did take different routes getting there!

Most adults walk that straight line every day. We

have obligations and bills to pay. We have much to accomplish in little time. We wake up and just hope we can keep putting one foot down in front of the other long enough to make it through the work day.

Dogs, on the other hand, move forward by going sideways, or even backward at times. They are led by smells and curiosity. By the wind, or the feel of the ground under their paws. Or the prospect of rolling in the sand or meeting up with a new four-legged friend. They set out running in one direction only to stop and turn around for no apparent reason other than to revisit something behind them.

I first noticed this behavior years ago when our golden retriever, Bido, was still alive. My husband and I would often take him for walks at a greenway near our house. On quiet days we would remove his leash and he would take off through the woods like a hyena with its hair on fire.

We, of course, followed the path set out in front of us. We knew he would reappear when it was time to load up and go home, and he always did. Sometimes caked in mud or smelling of carrion, but he always showed up with a smile on his sweet face.

I found myself envying those carefree dogs that morning on the beach. You see, I am a person who likes structure, so much so that if I am not careful, I will schedule my day down to the minute. I am not particularly fond of surprises or sudden changes of plan. I like to make my bed first thing in the morning and put things in their proper place. I have goals and think the quickest, easiest, and most time-efficient way to achieve them is by following that straight line.

But the prints I saw in the sand that weekend reminded me that I can still end up where I want to go even if I take a curvier, more creative path. I learned that I can afford the time to explore something new, even if it's on a side road. I can afford the time to revisit something behind me on occasion. I can afford to be curious.

Those meandering footprints in the sand taught me that I can live with joyous abandon at times and still arrive at my destination. Just like dogs do.

The Flexibility Factor

When it comes to not trying yoga, the king of excuses is "I'm just not flexible!" Oh, I've heard other excuses, of course, but I would have become a rich woman by now if I had gotten a dollar every time I heard that phrase over the years.

When people hear that you are a yoga teacher, it's like they have to explain to you why they *can't* do yoga. Now, I know yoga is a tough sell to a lot of people, and I long ago realized that encouraging people to at least try yoga is a delicate art. I am a soft-sell type of yoga teacher. I figure people will either eventually come around to yoga or they won't. I don't take it personally. I'm not going to push them and I definitely will not think any less of them if they choose not to take my class. Or any yoga class, for that matter.

The excuses people use say a lot more about them than they realize, though. This "lack-of-flexibility" excuse is one that reveals something about a person, and it has nothing to do with their tight hamstrings. After all, one of the main reasons people choose to do yoga in the first place is to *improve* their physical flexibility. Being flexible is not a prerequisite. You become more flexible *after* you begin practicing yoga. As a matter of fact, it's the people with tight hamstrings and hips and shoulders that benefit from yoga the most!

I believe that when people play the "lack-of-flexibility" card, they are really exposing a *mental* lack of flexibility, not a *physical* one. Not being open to new experiences. Allowing fears or phobias to block them from bettering their health and well-being. Perhaps they don't want to look inexperienced among their peers. Or they think that others will judge them. And let's face it, who wants to expose themselves to all of that?

What I wish I could tell these "inflexible" people is that those who attend yoga classes are there to take care of their own business. What you do or don't do in class affects no one there but you. You can look at people in class all you want to, but their effort doesn't change you. YOUR effort changes

you.

After years of practicing yoga, I have, indeed, become more flexible. I can touch my toes. I can do a backbend. I *love* the pigeon pose. But the part of my body that has benefited the most from all this stretching is my mind. I have stretched myself out of my comfort zone many times and not only survived but thrived.

Yoga represents challenges, both real and imaginary. When you stretch yourself in class, you provide yourself with viable mental tools to use in the real world. You become more pliable in thought and creativity. You stop assuming that you can't do something just because you've never done it before. You become more willing and able to take care of your own business.

In truth, the *real* benefits of yoga are seen and experienced off the mat. In the real world. In YOUR real world. Can I guarantee that you'll be able to touch your toes one day? No, I can't. But I *can* guarantee that, with practice, you'll cultivate your flexibility and get closer than you ever have before.

Flipping the Comparison Coin

Flipping the comparison coin is risky business. If the coin lands on one side you could be inspired, invigorated, and focused toward your goal. But if it lands on the other side you could be plunged into the depths of jealousy and low self-esteem.

Is it possible to guarantee that your coin will land on the more positive side?

I think teachers (and parents and leaders) of all disciplines wrestle with this monster at some point during their careers. I have witnessed this coin tossing many times in the yoga studio, and it can get ugly when the coin lands on the wrong side. Students too often get bogged down in "I'll never be as flexible as so-and-so, she has more arm strength than I do so why should I even try to do crow, I can't do a headstand like him so I must suck, etc."

One of the most common expressions you will hear in a yoga class is "respect your body." Usually, this phrase means to not push too hard in a particular posture or force the body past its natural resistance point. Now, don't get me wrong, these are important things to remember when practicing any physical discipline or sport.

But I think what we should be saying as teachers instead of "respect your *body*," is "respect your *person*." To respect your *person* encompasses the entirety of the physical, mental, and emotional aspects of ourselves. I believe if a student respects their whole person, their comparison coin will most of the time land positive side up. Why is this?

When a student respects their entire person, they are more likely to respect the entire person that is the object of comparison as well. When you compare yourself to another person from the perspective of respect, that means the two of you are on equal footing. One is not better than the other, just different.

From this place of equality, you are then allowed to admire without jealousy, appreciate without judgment, and emulate without fear of failure. And, as a bonus, you realize that both objects of comparison are capable of bettering

themselves with dedication, practice, and patience.

Instead of feeling jealous that your neighbor can touch her toes in class, why not flip the coin and be inspired by the capacity of the human body to stretch with practice?

Instead of despairing over not being able to go up into a headstand like that guy over there in the corner, why not be happy there is something in his hectic life he can control? There are many other ways to exercise control than by turning yourself upside down, but you can use his headstand as a springboard to creatively address the lack of control you may feel in your own life.

Instead of getting angry that everyone else in the class can do the dancer posture except you, why not appreciate the beauty and grace of the pose? Isn't it fantastic to be able to find beauty in another's efforts? Do you see how inspiring that can be? After all, that person is just as human and mortal as you are, so does it not then make sense that you have the capacity to move in that positive direction as well?

I guarantee you that no one walks into a yoga class just magically being able to do these fantastical asanas. Yoga is a skill-based practice, with the emphasis on *practice*. So to compare

yourself negatively to someone who has put in the hours of effort is not only not fair to you, it diminishes their hard work.

As human beings, we will never be able to get away from comparing ourselves to others because it's inherent in our nature. But if you flip the comparison coin and it ends up on the negative side, know that you always get a do-over. You can flip that coin again and focus on the positive side instead!

It's your choice whether to be discouraged by the achievements of others or to be inspired by the capacity of human beings to succeed and better themselves.

A Quote on Giving

I am a quote collector. Always have been. I kept a quotes notebook when I was a teenager, mostly recording memorable passages from books I was reading at the time. I wish I still had that little notebook, but it was lost during one of the many moves in my life. These days I keep meaningful quotes I find in a file I keep on my computer. And, of course, the occasional sticky note.

I love quotes for a number of reasons. It's comforting to me to know that even though a person is dead, their thoughts are still alive. Quotes remind me that there have always been deep thinkers and dreamers, and I am amazed that words spoken or written hundreds of years ago could still be relevant today. Could have meaning for ME. Could speak to me directly as if calling through a

time tunnel.

When I come across a good quote, I often chew on it for many days, meditate on it, relish it. I came across a quote by Longfellow one week not long ago that stuck with me: "Give what you have to somebody, it may be better than you think."

I find myself still drawn to this one.

Maybe it's because it speaks to my fear of not being good enough. Not believing my contributions have merit or will mean anything to anyone else.

Now, we have no problem offering our material stuff. How many loads of used clothes (holes and all) have we dropped off at Goodwill? They aren't good enough for us anymore, but they are better than nothing for people who have nothing. It's all relative, right? Surely they will appreciate our worn boots and dented pots and pans.

We never know who will receive our donations or if our discarded stuff will help them, but we give anyway and assume the goods will end up where they need to go.

But when it comes to offering bits of ourselves, we aren't so bold. We often keep our artistic and creative endeavors hidden for fear they won't be good enough. We don't speak up because we don't think anyone will want to hear what we have to

say. We don't reach out to other people for fear of rejection, thinking we don't have what they need or want.

This quote by Longfellow reminds me that we are the worst judges of our own value. How can I know if my writing will ever mean anything to anyone? It may not be perfect, but it may be what someone needs to read today. Or in two hundred years. After all, Longfellow had no way of knowing that his words would touch a middle-aged woman living in South Carolina in the twenty-first century. Who am I to judge what might speak to someone else?

I mean, how arrogant is that? What right do I have to decide what someone else might need or want? What might have meaning for them?

So I say go create something. Find your voice. Put it out there, into the world of hungry people. Give your art as freely as you give your tattered jeans. Contribute. Give what you have. Give your talents, your thoughts, your deeds, and trust your goods will end up where they need to go, will touch who they need to touch. After all, your contributions just might be better than you think.

Daily Differences

Did you know that you will never again have the exact same body that you have today? Most people get out of bed in the morning and just assume they will pick up where they left off yesterday, physically speaking, with no discernible differences. But the things we do one day can dramatically affect our bodies the following day and into the future.

Add in all the things we go through in our lifetimes (injuries, accidents, childbirth, illnesses, divorce, abuse, and addictions, just to name a few) and it's easy to understand that our physical bodies are in constant flux just to keep us up and running.

Sometimes, after a period of consistent exercise, we notice that we are getting stronger and improving our physical selves. We feel great when

these changes are of a positive nature.

But we are also faced with times of decline, either from external or internal forces, or from choices we have made along the way. This is where our physical and emotional selves can take a beating.

I hear it all the time: I could do a split when I was a child, I could touch my toes before I injured my back, I didn't have this problem before I had children, etc. We all have good days and bad days, feeling absolutely fine one morning, only to wake up the next morning with that old high school football injury flaring up, or an infection setting in where we cut our finger chopping onions the night before.

Not recognizing our present selves as different from the earlier models of ourselves is something we all struggle with at some point in our lives, whether or not we practice yoga. I used to think my body would always do what I wanted it to do, would always be the same. But that was before a car accident in college busted my left knee to pieces and left me with chronic hip problems. I've heard similar stories from my students over the years.

Yoga has helped me personally address the daily

differences and changes in my own life because every time I step on the mat I am presented with a slightly different version of myself. I didn't understand this at all when I first began studying yoga. As a result, I would do the same postures the same way every time, assuming that my body would respond exactly the way it did the last time I practiced.

I didn't take into account the time of day I was practicing (morning time is peaceful for the mind but the body tends to be less flexible) or the fact that I had just hiked five miles the day before (meaning that my legs were tired!).

But gradually, the longer I practiced on the mat, the more I learned to respect how different my body can be from one day to the next. I learned not to assume *anything* about my body because when I did, I ended up pushing my body past its limit, sometimes to the point of injury.

Just because I did a backbend yesterday is no guarantee I will be able to do one today. Because I was able to sit calmly in *virasana*, the hero, a week ago does not ensure that my knees will like it today. Through the years I have gained postures and lost postures, and, as a result, I've learned to hold on to them loosely.

My yoga practice has directly influenced how I interpret and live my life off the mat because it is not only our physical selves that change every day. Our emotional selves undergo changes on a daily basis, too.

I have learned that it is not always true that we emotionally step in a forward direction. There are days when I feel totally in control and strong. But if I see or experience something that reminds me of a difficult time in my life, I often become like a child again, and struggle to hold on to the lessons I thought I had already mastered.

My work on the mat has proven to me that I can't "fix" something one time and call it done. I am constantly in tune-up mode, which is how I now approach my emotional self as well.

One of my goals as a teacher in the studio is to help my students work with and respect the body they have *today*, not the one they had yesterday or ten years ago. Once we accept the fact that we are ever-changing beings and decide to courageously meet ourselves honestly each day, we become free to explore life outside the oppressive boundaries of assumption.

Three Things You Absolutely, Positively Do NOT Have to Have to Practice Yoga

I often receive emails from people who are interested in attending yoga classes, and along with the usual questions about class times and prices, I am almost always asked 1) do I need a mat, and 2) what should I wear. The truth is, no, and whatever you want.

The yoga industry has blossomed into a huge and expanding business where mind-boggling amounts of dollars are spent every year. And while I understand a person's enthusiasm in wanting to have the latest and greatest yoga gear, the truth is that many of the things we think we absolutely have to have, we really don't need at all, or at least don't

need to spend an exorbitant amount of money on.

Here are three things that you absolutely, positively, do NOT have to have to practice yoga.

A Yoga Mat

What do you mean I don't need a yoga mat? Doesn't *everyone* need a yoga mat?

Considering that people have been practicing yoga for over 5000 years and the yoga "sticky" mat wasn't invented until the early 1980's, I'd say that a yoga mat is not really a necessity.

For many years, yogis have practiced on the earth, on dirt, grass, and sand. If you are indoors, you can practice on the bare floor or even on carpet. I have known people to practice on beach towels, throw rugs, and blankets.

So why do we have yoga mats, and do they serve any purpose at all?

Yoga mats were developed to reduce slipping while practicing standing postures, and also to provide a degree of padding on our sensitive tushes and knees while in seated or kneeling postures. And, I'll admit, those are pretty good reasons.

I, myself, usually do practice on a mat. I like the ritual of rolling my mat out because it reminds me

that I am transitioning from a hectic world to a more serene one.

But I have also practiced on the beach, in the airport, and standing in the middle of my husband's garden with not a mat in sight. Not having a mat is not a valid excuse for avoiding yoga. Ask the thousands, if not millions, of yogis that studied yoga before 1980.

Yoga clothes

If you play football, you have to wear a uniform because you need your pads and helmet for protection. Basketball players wear shorts for ease of movement and because let's face it, it gets hot running up and down the court. Study judo and you will wear a gi because you need to be able to grasp your opponent's clothes to execute certain moves.

So what is the standard yoga uniform?

There is none. You can practice yoga in your sweatpants. Or your pajamas. Really, all you need to wear to practice yoga are comfortable clothes that don't restrict your movement. That's it! Heck, some people even practice in the nude.

I usually wear "yoga" clothes when I teach so that students can better see my form when I

demonstrate postures. But I have practiced yoga in a bathing suit, in dress pants, even one time in a cocktail dress. I love practicing in my jammies when it's cold.

Not having fancy yoga clothes is not an excuse to skip yoga. Wear what you want, and get on with it!

Props (straps, blocks, bolsters)

I will start this section by saying that incorporating props into a yoga practice is a good thing for many people. The use of props is one of the ways B. K. S. Iyengar was able to make the ancient practice of yoga accessible to the masses. But the fancy, expensive props you find in most yoga studios are simply not a necessity at home.

Looking for a block? How about that old phone book, a small step stool, or even a left over brick from your last renovation project instead?

Need a strap? I usually use one of my husband's old neckties as a strap. In a pinch, I have also used a piece of rope, a kitchen towel, even a sock one time while on vacation.

Your restorative pose calls for a bolster? We all have blankets and towels that will fit the bill. And

extra pillows from that rarely used guest room have always worked quite nicely for me.

Sorry, but not having the latest purple or green foam or cork block or that cool tapestry-covered bolster from India is not a good excuse for not practicing your yoga. Period.

All you *really* need to bring to your yoga practice is a desire to better yourself, one breath at a time.

Things I Learned While Cleaning My Mini Blinds

After living in Ecuador for three years, my husband and I (and our two cats) decided it was time to return to the States. We procured a cute little house in a cute little neighborhood in South Carolina.

We really loved the house, but while the previous owners did a great job with the big things, like remodeling the kitchen, replacing flooring, painting, etc., they overlooked some of the little things. Like cleaning the mini blinds.

Now, once a person knows something, they cannot "un-know" it. So once I knew how dirty the mini blinds were, I just couldn't "un-know" how dirty the mini blinds were. After a few choice words

that made my cat blush, I set out to clean all eleven less-than-pristine mini blinds.

This did not make me happy.

I mean, here I was in a new house and there were "sexier" jobs I was looking forward to, like picking out bedding and organizing the closets. But a funny thing happened when I started cleaning the blinds. I actually learned some things. Things about my new house. Things about my new neighborhood. And things about me.

I learned that kitchen blinds really do get funky. All that grease attracts dirt and dust like a neodymium magnet. I started with the kitchen blinds and swore if all the blinds in the rest of the house were that difficult to clean I would strip them down and burn them in the backyard. Luckily, there was only one set of blinds in the kitchen, and once I learned the others would not be quite as difficult to tackle, I calmed down a bit.

I learned that the sun rises at the front of the house. This nugget of information made me re-evaluate the window treatments I had been considering.

I learned that just because you can't see something doesn't mean it doesn't exist. When we moved in, all the blinds were closed, which is not

unusual in the south during the hot months; it was September and South Carolina was still sweltering. But this meant I couldn't really see the backyard from inside the house. When I opened the blinds on the back door to clean them, I noticed how very wonderful our backyard was. Private and pretty with several tall oaks, and there was a great open spot that would be perfect for my husband's future garden.

I learned that at least one lanky teen likes to skateboard barefooted down our street. I took a short break to watch him, and he looked so peaceful with the wind gently tousling his sandy hair as he glided from one side of the street to the other. Made me want to go check out the latest decks and trucks.

I learned that a family of deer lives nearby and likes to romp in our yard. A daddy, mama, and twins. Great for me because I love watching them play. Not so great for my husband's garden.

I learned there are no windows on the south side of the house.

I relearned that there are leash laws in the States. I had forgotten this because there are no leash laws in Ecuador.

I learned that most of the neighbors in my new

neighborhood take their dogs with them on their walks, and I saw many sizes and breeds of dogs, all with really cute and colorful walking accouterments. *And* they clean up the poop. The neighbors, not the dogs.

I learned that there is a big difference between plastic and metal mini blinds, especially while cleaning them. The metal ones bend and crease. Permanently. Remember that if you ever clean metal mini blinds. You're welcome.

I learned that after living in a South American city where people fix something at least a dozen times before replacing it that it is not easy to throw things away. I had a couple of friends say that they would have tossed the offensive blinds right out and gotten new ones. But I just couldn't do it. Now I understand why people who lived through the Great Depression saved everything. It's all right, I'm laughing at me, too, but I did save enough money by not replacing the blinds to buy several really nice bottles of wine. Doesn't sound quite so crazy now, does it?

I learned that at about three in the afternoon the shadows cast by the sun through the trees make a really beautiful filigree pattern across the lawn, like lovely lace.

I learned that the advice given in the Churchill and Morey tune from Snow White and the Seven Dwarfs, "Whistle While You Work," actually has merit. "It won't take long when there's a song to help you set the pace." I found that humming "La Marseillaise" did, indeed, make the work go faster. Why the French national anthem? Beats me. On the second day, it was "Shake Your Groove Thing" by Peaches and Herb. Hey, don't judge me. On the third day, it was "Ode to Joy" from the fourth movement of Beethoven's Ninth Symphony. See, I do have a little class after all.

Perhaps the biggest thing I learned from three days of cleaning filthy blinds is that I can follow my own advice. I always tell my yoga students that they don't have to do every part of every posture all at once, that they can break things down into smaller chunks and build the posture over time, step by step.

I cleaned the blinds in small sections, taking the time to stop and clean my cloth every so often, and by the second day I had really gotten into a rhythm. It was then I realized I had a great opportunity to use this chore as a meditation.

Once I applied that thinking to my work, everything changed. I became less resentful and

more at peace with the cleaning job ahead of me. I began to enjoy the repetition, the feel of the cloth in my hand, the scent of the cleaning solution.

After all these years, I am still amazed at how many times yoga has made my life off the mat more enjoyable and more productive. All I needed was a few dirty mini blinds to remind me!

Yoga Found Me. Again.

Most of us "yoga people" find yoga by seeking it out, by attending classes and practicing the postures. We find yoga by reading books and going to weekend workshops and reading the popular blogs. By following the newest yogi phenom on YouTube or listening to meditation podcasts in the carpool line. There is no shortage of ways to find yoga in this digital age.

But I am here to tell you that sometimes it's OK to let yoga find you.

The first time yoga found me was about two years after I began studying yoga. I had just had major surgery and recovery was not easy. I spent most of the first month after my surgery in bed trying not to become depressed and discouraged at the slow pace of recovery. The discomfort was

difficult to manage those first days and weeks, and I experienced bad side effects from the pain meds.

One day when I was on the verge of breaking down, yoga found me. It gracefully slipped into my room and encouraged me to breathe deeply into the pain. It taught me how to essentially massage the affected area with the movement of my breath.

I became calmer, even fascinated at how I could reach deeper into the body with just my breath and attention. Mind you, I wasn't all of a sudden miraculously pain-free, but I did learn how to better manage my situation without becoming panicked or hopeless.

The second time yoga found me, I was struggling to forge a new life for myself after a divorce. I made some bad decisions and felt very alone and lost most of the time, even though I had wonderful and supportive family and friends.

Yoga found me hungover in bed one morning and insisted that I get up and go to my mat. I obeyed. And I continued to go to the mat consistently over the following weeks and months, getting my life back on track, putting myself in a better frame of mind to meet my current husband and re-establishing the discipline that keeps me sane and happy.

The next time yoga found me, I was in Ecuador. My husband and I had lived in the country for several years with no problems, but one day I woke up with a wicked case of the Ecuadorian flu. I had a fever, chills, backache, joint pain, and a cough so deep, it hurt my kidneys. I basically lived in a tight fetal position under four Andean alpaca blankets for the better part of a week while my sweet husband waited on me hand and foot.

The first day, yoga stayed away. It wisely left my fever and coughing fits to try and sort themselves out. My body had to have time to assess the invader and come up with some type of a game plan.

The second day, my achy muscles were tightening and collapsing inward, contracting from the shivering fetal position I had been in for so long. It was then that yoga took the opportunity to quietly ease into bed with me.

Yoga reminded me that I could direct my shallow, cough-infused breath into my back. Inhale-2-3-4, exhale-2-3-4. I could feel my lungs gently expanding, allowing a brief respite from the violent hacking that had become my new norm.

The third day I knew I had to get out of bed before my hips and back got...well, stuck. Yoga found me sitting on the edge of the bed with

humped shoulders, still coughing like mad. But yoga encouraged me to slowly go down to the floor and get into child's pose. Then it listened to the feedback my body provided and guided me into a couple of cat/cow stretches, a very lopsided pigeon, and eventually asked that I place my legs up the wall for a few minutes before I crawled back in bed, where, thankfully, I was finally able to release the grip of the oppressive fetal position.

People wonder why I am so passionate about sharing yoga with my classes and through my books. This is why. If you are ever so low that you cannot find yoga, there's a good chance that yoga will find you.

The Evolution of a Yoga Posture

When I first started practicing yoga, I often said, "I can't do that!" Now, after two decades of practicing, studying, and teaching yoga, I say, "I can't do that. YET." Why the yet at the end?

Because I believe in evolution.

Apart from the Darwinian meaning of the word evolution, Merriam-Webster defines evolution as "a process of slow change and development." The Free Dictionary says evolution is "a gradual process in which something changes into a different and usually more complex form."

Slow change. A gradual process. You get the picture.

In my own personal practice and in teaching, I have experienced two main types of yoga evolution. The first is the slow change I experience

while in a posture during one practice session. The other is the gradual transformation of a posture over an extended period of time.

Yoga, like most worthwhile endeavors, is a skill-based practice. Progress is naturally built into the process if you stay the course. I'll use *adho mukha svanasana*, or downward facing dog, as an example.

Let's say that Sue goes to a yoga class one day. The teacher eventually guides the class into downward facing dog. Sue gets herself into position, but this is a hard one for her. She has a rounded back and her wrists hurt in this posture every time. Her heels aren't anywhere near the floor and she can't straighten her legs.

So the teacher comes over and offers a few suggestions. She asks that Sue really spread her fingers far apart so that she can feel all four corners of her palms pressing down, especially that stubborn mound at the base of the index fingers. Maybe she could nudge her chest a little more in the direction of her toes to help take some pressure off her wrists and bring awareness to her thoracic spine. She could also strengthen her thigh muscles more and press them toward the back of the room, encouraging her legs to shift back a little bit, even if

they don't totally straighten.

These are small tweaks to the posture, but the posture Sue ends with at the end of class is different from the one she started with. Her posture has evolved over the course of **one class**.

Sue continues attending yoga classes.

Two years later, the teacher guides the class into *adho mukha svanasana*. This time Sue's palms are wide and flat on her mat. Her back is longer and her legs are almost straight. Her heels still don't go all the way down to the floor, but they are closer than they were in the earlier class mentioned above.

So, the teacher comes over and offers a few suggestions. Perhaps Sue could encourage her inner thighs to reach further back while gently nudging her sit-bones away from each other. Instead of just pressing her palms down, maybe she could also press them in a forward direction against her mat while she moves her tailbone in the direction of where the wall and the ceiling meet behind her. Her outer hips could lift up while her heels continue to press down.

Again, based on where Sue started in the posture this time, these are relatively small tweaks. But they are very different adjustments from those

two years ago because her posture has evolved **over time**. She has been diligent in her practice and has gained skills along the way. And if she keeps practicing, these skills will continue to multiply. In two more years, the suggestions Sue will receive from her teacher will be different still. This is how a posture evolves.

Slow change. A gradual process.

In my own life, I can't do the full yoga peacock. YET. I can't play the tricky third movement of Beethoven's Moonlight Sonata. YET. I can't fold an origami dragon. YET. But I know if I continue honing my skills, these things are possible.

So instead of thinking that you can't do something, realize that you just may not be able to do it YET. And know that when you are focused and diligent, YET arrives sooner than you think.

A Quote on Genius

I've come to the conclusion that no one can avoid the work. And lots of it. It doesn't matter if you're gifted or brilliant. High IQ? Doesn't matter. You still have to do the work.

I came across this quote by Michelangelo recently and I haven't been able to get it out of my mind.

"If you knew how much work went into it, you would not call it genius."

It took over two years for one of the most revered artistic geniuses in history to complete his statue of David. But the fact he was a genius didn't mean he didn't have to do the work. He still had to work the marble, day after day, month after month, just so the "genius" would have a chance to pop out one day through the rock.

As well as teaching yoga, I also teach piano and composition. Not long ago I was working with one of my adult piano students on analyzing one of the Bach Two-Part Inventions. I pointed out where the first key change occurred, and then showed her how Bach had painstakingly set up that change several measures beforehand using a type of musical foreshadowing. She looked at me and said, "Do you think composers think about this stuff when they write music?"

Not only do they think about this stuff, they *work* on this stuff. Constantly. They work to improve their craft, to tighten their skills, to hone their understanding of form so their musical ideas will have the best chance of shining through, like David emerging from the marble.

Still not convinced, she said, "But can't somebody write something good without knowing all these technical things?"

"Of course, they can," I said. "They're called one-hit wonders."

Sometimes people do get lucky and produce a truly beautiful piece of art or lovely piano sonata. But if they don't continue learning, working hard, digging deeper, and improving their understanding of their craft, they will never be placed on the

"genius" pedestal. They will simply be someone who got lucky.

The truth is, Pulitzer prize-winning novels don't write themselves and masterpiece sculptures don't magically appear from stone. We may not see the artist's effort, but it's always there. You cannot avoid the work. And lots of it.

Even if you are a genius.

Your Yoga Toolbox

After years of diligent practice, I am amazed at how full my yoga toolbox has become. I started collecting yoga tools with my first class, although I didn't really know how or when to use those tools in my real life at the time. That came later. But I believe that consistent use of these yoga tools through the years has helped me build a better me, both physically and emotionally.

So what yoga tools can help you in your day-to-day life? When should you reach into your yoga toolbox?

When you want to improve your flexibility

Most people come to yoga because they hear it will help them improve their flexibility, especially

in their hamstrings. Yoga can also help with tight hips, knees, and shoulders. LeBron James credits yoga for improving his flexibility, which alleviates muscle cramps and reduces the occurrence of injuries on the basketball court. Not a bad endorsement!

Your hamstrings need a good stretch? Reach into your toolbox and pull out a downward facing dog or a good ole standing forward bend. Want to increase the range of motion in your knees? How about a bound angle posture or hero's pose? Tight hips? Grab a pigeon, a happy baby, and a half lord of the fishes. Battling chest constriction? The locust is a great way to open the chest as well as stretch the fronts of the shoulders.

When you want to work on your strength

Yoga isn't just about flexibility. Use the right yoga tools and you can quickly boost the strength in your arms, legs, and abdominals.

Want to banish those flabby arms? Dolphin planks, the four-limbed staff pose, and crow are tools that will get you on your way to lean, strong arms. Want to strengthen your legs and ankles? Reach into your toolbox and pull out any of the

standing postures. Seriously. *Any* of them. Your belly not quite a six-pack? Hard to beat a good boat, plank, or half moon.

When you need to calm down

Yoga tools aren't just for use on the mat. When you are stressed, no matter what the reason, know that there are yoga techniques that can help you refocus your mind and lower your blood pressure.

Whether you are stressed at work or the kids are driving you nuts, sometimes the only tool you need is your breath. Nice thing is, it doesn't have to be complicated! Simply taking a few slow, deep, and deliberate breaths that extend all the way down to your belly will help lower blood pressure and calm you right down.

I reach for the breath tool a lot when I am about to say something I might regret!

When you need help losing weight

We, as a society, are way too obsessed with weight. But there are legitimate health concerns to consider when someone is obese. Is there a yoga tool for weight loss?

Yes! But the key is consistency. You can't just go to one class and expect to lose weight.

One of the ways yoga helps with weight loss is by making a person more aware of his or her body and what is being put into it. Some great yoga tools for weight loss are the eating meditations, like the Taste and Tracing Origin meditations. I describe these meditations in depth in my book *How to Sneak More Meditation Into Your Life*. These tools will not only help you slow down the eating process, which will help you eat less, but will compel you to consider where your food comes from and what it's really made of.

When you have back pain

Chronic back pain is, unfortunately, very common in adults. Luckily, yoga offers many ways to address releasing and relaxing the back as well as strengthening the back and improving your posture. Many doctors are now prescribing yoga to their patients because it has been found so effective in combating back pain.

Got pain in your lower back? In your toolbox, you will find the cat/cow, child's pose, and *bharadvaja's* twist. Stiff between your shoulder

blades? Pull out an extended puppy pose and a locust posture. Wanting to improve back strength to help stave off back issues in the future? Grab a chair, a cobra, and a bridge.

When you want to improve your balance

Balance becomes more of a challenge as we age. Overwhelmingly, the majority of my students over the age of sixty say that falling is one of their greatest fears. Yoga can help you improve your balance, but it also makes you more aware of your environment so that you can better anticipate any rough patches ahead.

When you want to improve overall balance, the king of the balance postures is the tree. Tree teaches you to find and work with your center of gravity.

Technically, you can pull out any standing posture from your toolbox and you will be addressing balance. However, the standing twists, like the revolved triangle or the revolved half moon, are especially helpful.

Your yoga toolbox also contains non-standing balance postures, like the two-legged table, the boat, and all arm balances contribute to your overall coordination and balance.

When you want to improve your ability to concentrate

With so many distractions and everyone's propensity to multitask these days, our ability to focus has really suffered. So what does the yoga toolbox have for you on the concentration front?

When you find yourself battling a "monkey mind," take a deep breath and reach into your toolbox for a simple meditation technique. Again, this does not have to be difficult! You could spend several minutes simply following your breath, or you could try the counting backward meditation. Or practice a walking meditation, gaze at a candle for a few minutes, or concentrate on a sound. Or make a sound. As long as you bring your attention time and again to your object of concentration, you have succeeded in the battle against that hyper monkey!

Yoga is a diverse and rich practice that deepens over time, but one has to be willing to invest in these tools with practice, study, and application. Is it worth it? Ask the thirty million people practicing yoga across all backgrounds, nations, and cultures in the world right now if it's worth it to them, and

you will hear a resounding YES!

Building a better you *is* possible if you have the right tools and are willing to use them.

The Challenge of an
Accomplished Student

In the yoga world, teachers often don't know what to do with a student that swims into class being able to do sophisticated arm balances in a sea where the rest of the yogi fish are just trying to breathe. So what is a teacher supposed to do with one of these accomplished students?

While some teachers get a little flustered, I take another route. I choose to learn from them. Here are two examples from my own teaching experience and what I learned dealing with two very different accomplished students.

Years ago, I was getting ready for my mixed-level yoga class at a small YMCA in South Carolina. Now, a mixed-level class is just that, a class where

abilities and backgrounds differ, so one of the challenges as a teacher is to address everyone at his or her level. Having said that, a mixed-level class is not an advanced one, and most students range from beginner to intermediate.

Among the regulars that filtered into the class that day was a striking young woman I had never seen before. She looked like she could have been a prima ballerina with the Royal Ballet company. She arrived early and was poised and graceful as she quietly rolled out her mat near the back of the room. No one had any doubt whatsoever this chick would be able to touch her toes. Heck, she might even be able to reach China.

Curious eyes were glued to this woman as she slowly lifted herself up into a glorious downward facing dog for a few moments before lowering into a quiet hero pose, where she waited patiently for class to begin.

I went over to greet her, as I always do with new students, so that I could find out if she had any physical issues or illnesses I needed to be aware of before starting class. She had indeed been a dancer, but suffered some lingering effects from that strenuous profession and had come to yoga to slow down and to relearn as a "civilian" how to keep her

body flexible and strong as she aged. I welcomed her and started class.

As I began guiding the class through some introductory postures, I noticed that the other students couldn't stop glancing in the dancer's direction. Understandable, really, because she was beautiful to watch, even in the most basic of postures.

She was very deliberate in her approach to the poses we went over that day, and I soon realized that I had the perfect opportunity to use this beautiful specimen to point out some things in a three-dimensional way to my other students.

You see, during the course of a class, I often stop to physically demonstrate things I believe can help my students as they are trying to learn a posture. But sometimes I wish I had a blackboard (and drawing skills) because it is difficult to point out something on the back side of your body!

Luckily, this young woman was willing to be my model and I was able to hone in on some of the intricacies of a forward bend, as well as some of the things that people need to keep in mind as their flexibility improves. And while the new student was fantastic with everything on two feet that day, she struggled with the balance postures due to an ear

infection. Seeing that lovely creature flail in tree was a great lesson for the class because it demonstrated that you really do have a different body every day!

This accomplished student was only in town for a weekend visiting relatives, so I did not see her in class again. But because of her giving attitude and willingness to be part of a community, we all learned something that day.

My students learned that even former ballerinas have bad balance days and that *everyone* has to work at maintaining their body. I learned from her the importance of staying with a posture all the way through the release and began right away incorporating that nugget into my own practice as well as my teaching.

Fast-forward several years. I was now teaching yoga in a lovely city in South America where people tended to come and go a lot. Of course, I would have regulars, but they were inclined toward travel and adventure in their retirement, so the mix of attendees was in constant flux.

I was well into my class one afternoon when in waltzed a beautiful young woman who proceeded to throw her belongings against the back wall before unfurling her mat with a loud whip on the

front row. She then went about her own business, never once following along with the rest of the class, not interested in the least in what I was teaching.

The class was a beginner's class and here she was on the front row doing advanced standing postures, arm balances, splits, and headstands. Her body control was impressive and some of her postures would make a gymnast jealous; however, not once did I consider using her as an example for the rest of the class.

Her inconsideration of the class setting was baffling, and I wondered why she had bothered coming to class in the first place if she was just going to do her own thing. I had even exchanged a couple of emails with her earlier that week about what type of class it would be, time, etc., and she assured me that she was fine with a slower-paced beginner's class.

But I learned something from that young woman that day. I learned that even when one's posture is over-the-moon gorgeous, if it is not practiced with humility, it can quickly turn disruptive and ugly.

Learning is about gaining knowledge and insight, not showing off what you already know. That is what performances are for, and yoga is a

PRACTICE, not a performance.

Fortunately, if you have the right mindset, you will learn something in every situation, as I did in both examples above. I value both of those experiences equally (even though one was more pleasant than the other) because I was able to learn from each accomplished student something that I could take forward with me as a teacher, and as a practitioner.

How Yoga Helped Me Rehab My Frozen Shoulder

"But you can't have a frozen shoulder. You do yoga!"

I heard this from some of my friends a while back after I was diagnosed with a frozen shoulder. But even a dedicated yogini can get a frozen shoulder. I'm living proof.

Now, if you aren't familiar with this shoulder affliction, yay! I hope you never have to deal with it. Frozen shoulder is one of those really weird medical conditions that seems to appear out of nowhere and is hard to detect because it creeps up on you.

The really frustrating thing is no one can tell you why you ended up with it. Not the doctor. Not the

physical therapist. No, not even the almighty Google can tell me why I got a frozen shoulder. But I did.

Frozen shoulder most commonly affects women between the ages of forty and sixty, although men are not immune to the condition. It *could be* the result of a previous or recent injury. It *could be* related to diabetes. It *could be* virus related. It *could be* a hormone imbalance. It *could be* because you didn't move enough after a surgery. It *could be* because you got up on the wrong side of the bed. OK, I made that last one up. The truth is no one knows why some people develop a frozen shoulder and others don't.

So what is adhesive capsulitis, the fancy name for frozen shoulder? Basically, it's a condition where all the tissues around your shoulder shrink wrap themselves to the joint, which *severely* restricts your range of motion. Scar tissue forms, and then, my friend, you are in a heap of trouble.

Is it painful, you ask? The pain in my shoulder was unlike any pain I'd ever experienced in my life and brought me to my knees on more than one occasion. Yeah, it hurts.

So what does a person do if they develop a frozen shoulder? Well, they can wait several *years*

until it decides to clear up on its own, they can opt for physical therapy, or they can undergo a surgical procedure (while the patient is under a general anesthesia the surgeon goes in and "breaks" everything up...ouch!).

I chose the physical therapy route because 1) I am not a sit-around-and-wait kind of person, 2) I don't relish the idea of someone "breaking" parts of me while I am knocked out, and 3) I am already used to working with my body through yoga.

And by applying the following five yoga lessons to my physical therapy sessions, my body produced fantastic results in just a few weeks.

Yoga taught me to start where I am

Every time I step onto the yoga mat, I take a few moments to assess where I am that day, both physically and emotionally, because there are subtle (and sometimes not-so-subtle) differences in our bodies and minds from one day to the next.

Why is it important to take stock of ourselves before we practice yoga? Because when we take the time to check in with ourselves, we are better able to focus, and the chance we will sustain an injury while practicing is greatly reduced.

Because I am used to recognizing these daily physical and emotional shifts, I was able to honestly assess my shoulder situation when I began therapy. *Wanting* my shoulder to be completely healed was a great goal, but wanting it to be better didn't help me with a game plan. To develop a game plan, you have to know from what point you are starting.

I was starting from a place of damage, and that's just the way it was. Yoga helped me accept the starting line.

Yoga taught me you can't force things to happen

When I began studying yoga, I was already in my thirties and was dealing with some residual knee problems that stemmed from a car accident I had when I was in college.

One posture that appealed to me early on was *virasana*, the hero's pose. This is the one where you plop your bum down on the floor between your feet with both knees pointing ahead. Of course, that posture was impossible for me back then.

The couple of times I tried to force my body to go into *virasana,* it would have nothing to do with it and complained quite vehemently.

Once I left my obsession for this posture behind, though, and continued working on other aspects of the practice, my body gradually began easing in that direction. And one day, my knees allowed me to gently slide into the hero's pose with no fuss.

I knew I couldn't force my shoulder to get better. I could only do the work and know that one day my body would allow me to use my arm again, if not fully, then at least better than I could then. I knew it would happen because I had experienced that exact process and result before on the mat.

Yoga taught me to focus on the journey

This one may sound cliché, but it really is about the journey. Focus too long on the destination and you lose sight of all the interesting, infuriating, inspiring, and amazing things you pass along the way.

I had never had any problems whatsoever with my shoulders; I'll admit, I took them for granted. And even though this was a journey I never expected to have to take, I recognized that this was an opportunity to facilitate a palpable change in myself. I got to witness a damaged part become whole again, one baby step at a time.

And that's pretty awesome.

Yoga taught me to coordinate movement with breath

This was a biggie. When you coordinate movement with your breath, you become more mindful of what you are doing. Moving mindfully is ultimately how you get your body to trust you, trust that you are not trying to harm it further. Healing can't truly begin until this trust has been established.

Through yoga, I have learned to "play the edge," which secures this trust. I go into a posture as far as I comfortably can, then I focus all my attention and breath on the tightness and tension I feel. Inhalations keep me focused and expand the tight places, and exhalations allow me to release deeper into the posture. The release evolves over several breath cycles and can be quite dramatic.

I applied this principle to my shoulder therapy. Instead of holding a position for ten static seconds, I breathed through it for three full breaths, all the while focusing on trust and release with each exhalation. This was a game changer.

Yoga taught me to respect myself

On the mat, you learn to take everything in stride. So what if *urdhva dhanurasana* (the wheel, or full backbend) is not in my yoga repertoire at the moment? That doesn't mean I'm not a serious yoga person.

Not every body is capable of every posture, and that's what I love about the practice. We all bring something different to the mat, and it's all beautiful and valid.

So what if my shoulder didn't function properly for several months? This was not a reflection on me. Truth is, stuff happens in life, to all of us. It's how we deal with that stuff that matters, not the stuff itself.

So what were my fantastic results? Well, in less than three weeks after I began therapy I could wash my hair without wincing and I could get dressed without feeling like I just got the wind knocked out of me. I could put on my seatbelt with ease and I could pick up my cat again.

Now, I know that doesn't sound like much progress, but I assure you, it was miraculous to be able to once again perform simple daily tasks without breaking down in tears. And as I continued

improving over the following weeks and months, I considered myself lucky to have had the opportunity to be reminded just how precious these small moments in life really are.

Things I Learned from My Three-Legged Cat

My cat, Triplet, loves getting on the yoga mat with me every morning. Sometimes, I think she looks forward to it more than I do. I named her Triplet because a triplet is a musical term for a three-note rhythmic figure. You guessed it, this black cat only has three legs. Despite this handicap, and many other hurdles she's faced throughout the years, this little kitty has taught me a lot about life off the mat and how to handle tough situations with grace.

I don't know much about Triplet's past, except that it was pretty rough. She showed up under our back deck years ago so scrawny and pitiful, we almost didn't notice at first that one of her back legs

was missing. She picked our yard, one that already had a golden retriever and two other cats in it, so my husband and I knew that this poor feline must have been desperate. She could barely stand, and her skin drooped on her little skeleton like a man's coat does on a five-year-old playing dress up. She ate so fast when we fed her that she immediately threw up. She was a sad little kitty.

We thought she was a kitten at first because she was so tiny, but the vet said she was probably at least four years old. Her leg had been surgically removed and she had been spayed, so we knew at one time someone had cared for her. We contacted all the local vets and hung up signs hoping we would be able to find her owner, but no luck. No one was missing a starving, three-legged black cat. So after having a family pow wow with the other animals, we decided to keep the small vagabond.

From the beginning, it was pretty obvious Triplet had not been brought up around dogs. Our golden, Bido, was respectful of her, but he basically ignored her. And she never once tried to engage him or get his attention in any way. She seemed fine to go through life knowing that the canine of the family didn't care to play with her. This taught me that not everyone is always going to be into me, and that's

OK.

Triplet has a strange habit of eating plastic bags. We guess it's because she had to eat lots of garbage when she was surviving out on her own and probably equates plastic with food scraps. From observing this strange behavior, I learned that just because you *can* eat something doesn't mean you *should* eat it.

This little kitty of ours is handicapped, but that doesn't mean she doesn't contribute her available talents to the family. There are things she can't do, like jump on the kitchen counters, but plenty she can do. She catches flies if they fly low enough, and promptly disposes of them (by eating them). Same with other bugs and spiders. You see, just like any other cat, she likes to earn her keep. This taught me that we all have different capacities and *all* contributions are worthwhile.

When we lived in Ecuador, my husband brought home a scrawny gray kitten that he found on the way to the bus stop one morning. The new addition, Puck, *loved* his big sister right away. Big Sis, however, was not amused with the new addition and let us know straight away that she did not approve.

Now Puck, who grew into a hefty fella, has a

habit of sneaking up on poor Triplet. Triplet really hates this, but instead of attacking back, she simply moves on. This three-legged cat of ours has taught me that sometimes it's better to remove yourself from a bad situation than to expend pointless energy trying to combat it. Sometimes surviving the day is more important than winning the battle.

We are a society of excuse makers, and we are sorry for everything. But not Triplet. She makes no excuse for her handicap, and she never complains about not being able to jump on the counters. If she can pull herself up onto something, fine. If not, fine. I have learned that I do not need to feel sorry for her because her handicap is something that *happened* to her, and she is much more than the sum of her impediments. This taught me to really try to look past people's limitations and focus instead on the things they do bring to the table. This particular lesson has had a huge impact on my life.

When we moved back to the States, Triplet and I returned first to get the house set up while my husband and Puck finished up some business in Ecuador. Triplet had a grand time being the only cat in the house, so I was a little apprehensive about how she would react when she realized her arch enemy would be part of her life again.

After about a month, my husband and Puck joined us in the States. When we took Puck out of his carrier, Triplet walked right up to him, went nose to nose, and sniffed. No hissing, no defensive posturing, just some sniffing. She accepted him back right away. I had worried for nothing.

You see, just as we accept her and all of her limitations, she accepts him and all of his annoyances. After all, they are family. And that lesson is worth its weight in catnip.

Letting Go

I've learned many lessons practicing yoga through the years and I am thankful for the ones I've been able to apply to my real life once my mat has been rolled up and put away. Perhaps the most important lesson I've learned on this yoga journey of mine is what it means to let go.

Letting go can be tough. Letting go means you have to leave something behind: a situation, a project, an idea, a relationship, a loved one. And even though letting go of something usually means you are making room in your life for something else (hopefully something positive), that something else is most often an unknown quantity. And we don't like the unknown. The unknown can be scary.

Sometimes we are hesitant to let go because we simply don't know how. How does a person let go

of something in the first place? I'll admit I've had problems letting go of things in the past because I didn't know how to go about it, what to expect emotionally, or how to proceed afterward.

One of the first things we learn to do as students of yoga is to work with our breath. We practice pranayama (breathing exercises) to help us increase our lung capacity and learn that certain movements during asana practice can be enhanced if they are performed on either the inhalation or the exhalation.

Generally, backbends are approached with an inhalation, forward bends with an exhalation, and during twists, you lengthen the spine on the inhalation and twist on the exhalation. As with most things in life, there are exceptions to these rules, but if you follow those simple guidelines you will stay on track most of the time during your practice.

But what do you do when you are holding a posture and there is no movement to coordinate your breath with? This is where letting go comes into play.

Holding a yoga posture does not mean to hold the breath; we continue to breathe during asanas, either normally as some traditions suggest, or with a specific type of breath, like the Ujjayi breath used in

an Ashtanga practice. The one thing that remains the same regardless of the breathing method you use during your practice is that you want to try and facilitate a deeper release into the pose when you exhale.

Exhaling equals release. Exhaling equals letting go. Time after time, practice after practice, posture after posture, you have the opportunity to practice letting go.

So what is so important about learning to let go with the exhalation? Why is it with the exhalation that we release?

Our very first act as a human being is to inhale. The moment we emerge from the womb, it is our responsibility to take a deep breath in. No one can do this for us, we have to do it ourselves. We have to prove we have spunk and drive and want to be alive in the first place. And when we do, it is exhilarating and we have our whole lives in front of us. Inhaling represents expansion.

On the other hand, our last act as a human being is to exhale. We release our physical body with our last exhalation. Exhaling represents… letting go.

Conscious breathing during practice challenges a person to dig deeper, to breathe into the tension

on the inhalation and release that tension on the exhalation, to find the edge, to test the boundaries of life and death. Can this be scary? You bet.

But if you stick with the practice long enough, something really beautiful begins to happen. Something that teaches you letting go does not have to be so unnerving after all.

You see, there is a brief moment of time at the end of an exhalation, a time of stillness before the inhalation resumes the cycle. I used to be alarmed by this stillness. In fact, I used to shy away from it because it frightened me.

But what I found as I began to investigate this stillness further was that this space between the exhalation and inhalation produced a deep calmness in me, a sense of peace and tranquility. Being in this quiet place is like being safely submerged in a reflection pond where you can see everything clearly above you, yet nothing affects you in your serene space down below.

Yoga has taught me that if I want to live a peaceful, more meaningful life, I have to be willing to first let go. Let go of people who bring me down. Let go of situations that do not nourish my soul. Let go of expectations that hinder my progress on the road to becoming the best me I am capable of

becoming.

Letting go is an ongoing challenge, I'll admit. But by stepping onto my mat every day, I have the opportunity to practice again and again, breath after breath. I practice all kinds of things on my mat, really. When I practice yoga, I'm not just working on building a stronger and more self-confident me. I'm learning and relearning lessons I can use in my real life off the mat.

Just knowing I have this safe space to work on my yogini-in-progress has made all the difference in my life. So I return to my mat day after day, week after week, month after month, year after year...

Bonus!

An Excerpt from
How to Sneak More Yoga Into Your Life
by K. Kris Loomis

I never set out to study yoga. But when I did have the opportunity to explore yoga, I ran into the same problems that most people do after they've taken a few classes. I remember thinking, now what? I knew I needed to "practice," but had no idea how to begin. How do people improve if they don't have time to practice, or know HOW to practice in the first place? After many years of personal experience and teaching, I realized how easy it is to address this problem, so I wrote this book to share with you what has worked for me and many of my students.

My yoga journey began when a friend of mine invited me to go to a yoga class with her. She was a geriatric nurse and had read some studies about the benefits of introducing yoga therapy to older patients. She was interested in the possibility of boosting the quality of her patients' lives by helping them improve their stability and lung function.

To be honest, I wasn't really interested in yoga at that time, thinking it was a lot of new-age mumbo-jumbo. I envisioned a lot of hippies chanting while sitting in painful pretzel positions in a room stinking of incense. I did not think that scenario was for me, but I thought, at the worst, we would have a fun topic of conversation over a bottle of wine sometime. So I accepted her invitation.

The class was held at a local arts center by a quiet woman who was just beginning her teacher training. She did burn incense (not so "stinky" after all) but there would be no chanting that day. Among the vivid paintings of local Southern artists, the afternoon came to life with yoga dogs and frogs and trees and geometrical shapes that felt exhilarating and liberating to my tight muscles. I became dizzy from my breath. At one point I broke a sweat. This was not what I was expecting. I walked into that class a skeptic and walked out a student of yoga for

life.

I continued going to classes and began dabbling with yoga at home. I would try to recreate what we had done in class each week, but found, not only was it difficult to remember the postures and sequences, it was also difficult to find a decent block of time to practice. Inevitably, the phone would ring. My husband would walk through the room inquiring about dinner. My dog would plop down in the middle of my mat demanding a belly rub. And shouldn't I be putting that other load of clothes in the dryer?

After I started teaching, I heard similar complaints from my students. Seems that everyone these days is swamped with house stuff, kid stuff, garden stuff, relationship stuff, in-law stuff, with no time left for yoga stuff.

A couple of years passed, and I had not been able to give any better advice to my students than, "Just keep trying to set aside fifteen minutes a day." And, honestly, with a full-time job and teaching several yoga classes a week, I barely had time for my own practice. It was becoming more and more difficult for me to follow my own advice.

Then one day I began to realize that my yoga practice had started sneaking up on me away from

the mat. I would find myself in mountain pose while standing in line at the grocery store. I would automatically go into a seated twist if I had been at my desk too long. I instinctively altered my breath anytime I felt anxious or nervous. I found that five minutes were better than no minutes. And, in a pinch, even one minute would suffice.

Could it really be this easy to incorporate yoga into my hectic life? Could I count this as "practice?" Did yoga have to be a "separate" part of my life? The day I answered no to that last question was the day I started living my yoga. I now use every chance I get to sneak a little yoga in, no matter where or how busy I am. A little yoga is definitely better than no yoga!

I think that when we start studying yoga, we tend to focus on what we can't do rather than on what we can do. We see the pictures in magazines and websites of svelte yogis in impossibly difficult positions and forget that yoga is not about doing the difficult, but about doing something good for ourselves. I wrote this book so that you can see, with a few hacks and a willingness to try, how easy it is to integrate real yoga into your life. Not the kind that will wow the masses, but the kind that quantifiably contributes to your better physical and

mental well-being.

One Last Thing

Thank you for reading about my lessons learned on and off the mat! If you enjoyed *After Namaste: Off the Mat Musings of a Modern Yogini,* I'd be grateful if you would post a short review on Amazon. Your support and comments really make a difference, especially to indie authors!

I would also appreciate good old-fashioned "word of mouth" to your friends, colleagues, and anyone else you think might enjoy reading about how yoga can broaden your life even when you are away from the mat.

Thank you for reading my book!

About the Author

K. Kris Loomis is the author of two other books on yoga, *How to Sneak More Yoga Into Your Life: A Doable Yoga Plan for Busy People*, and *How to Sneak More Meditation Into Your Life: A Doable Mediation Plan for Busy People*.

Along with pursuing her lifelong dream of becoming a writer, Kris is a determined chess player, an origami enthusiast, a classically trained pianist, and a playwright. Kris lives in South Carolina with her husband and two cats (including Triplet, feline extraordinaire and star of Kris's humorous travelogue, *Thirty Days In Quito: Two Gringos and a Three-Legged Cat Move to Ecuador!*).

You can see Kris's current book selection, both

nonfiction and fiction, on her Amazon author page.

Visit Kris's website at www.kkrisloomis.com and receive a FREE short story! And you can find Kris on Facebook, Twitter, and Pinterest @kkrisloomis.